3

First published 2022

Copyright © Christopher Thomas King Hood 2022

The right of Christopher Thomas King Hood to be identified as the Author of this work has been asserted in accordance with the Copyright, Designs & Patents Act 1988.

All rights reserved. No part of this book may be reproduced, stored in a retrieval system, or transmitted in any form or by any means, electronic, electrostatic, magnetic tape, mechanical, photocopying, recording or otherwise, without the written permission of the copyright holder.

Published under licence by The Self-Publishing Partnership Ltd, 10b Greenway Farm, Bath Rd, Wick, nr. Bath BS30 5RL

ISBN printed book: 978-1-83952-559-9
ISBN e-book: 978-1-83952-560-5

Cover design by Kevin Rylands

Printed and bound in the UK

This book is printed on FSC® certified paper

Christopher Thomas
King Hood

Writer's note.

*I dedicate these writings to all those suffering with post-traumatic stress disorder.
Also to all the children who have been sexually abused, something I never witnessed personally, but see as a major problem in our society. Money from the sale of this book will be given to a child abuse service charity and to a military and civilian PTSD based charity. Creating awareness on these health crises is essential.*

*Also to my beautiful niece
Isla May.*

*May all who read have my love
along with great
health
wealth
and
happiness.*

Author's note

I am aware that some of my writings that you are about to read are of a gross and dark nature and might be scary and not pleasant for children to hear or read. So I declare this book to be read with parental consent.

Unfortunately some areas of our society are of a darker nature; this has been for many, many years.

Some of my stories are written in a symbolic nature and I advise to read them that way and try not to take it all too literally. I also recommend slowly reading the writings. A lot of it can be catchy with a lot of rhyming. You may find yourself trying to roll with it. Before you know it you may find yourself missing messages. So I apologise for my writing style. Remember patience is another life key to the universe.

Contents

Part 1: Awake   11

Part 2: The Dragon   55

Part 3: The Code   106

Part 4: The Symbol of 3   173

Part 1

Awake.

A brief food and exit introduction.

The emergency exit is located to the right,
eat and drink how you like,
but I suggest a healthy diet.
Sleep wherever you choose, please respect the dwelling you use.

Freedom is located inside of you.
I wish you all a pleasant journey.

Is everybody in?
Is that everybody who is ready, that's in?
Those who await an honest destiny,
will await the next room.
Ladies and gentleman, boys and girls.
My name is
Christopher Thomas King Hood
Born Friday 3rd April 1992
on a new moon,
an astrological view.

Dimensions, directions,
alignments, assignments,
understand symbols, understand life.

You may have come to read or listen today
because you are fed up of feeling insane,
disconnected or feeling in pain,
that only reigns,
because you have dimmed your flame.
I'm here to help compassionately ignite and protect your flame.
Or you may just be curious to see what I have to say.
My words may impose on your beliefs, but let's see what the next life choice can be.
Allow yourself to be open and ready,
one message maybe all you need,
but please feel free to be intrigued.
Once you have met the shamans and angels.
Wizards and magicians, allow yourself to see from any position.

Awake,
remember your dreams from your sleep
strong lion,
your love is awaiting a morning kiss.
The butterfly cries, the sign of your
morning yawn
you enter the kingdom at the break of dawn,
opening the doors with a morning roar
you roam the land in guardian, with the
black jaguars.
While the females, stag on duty,
guarding the universe, with Gods prophets and noble servants.
From the evil demons,
looking to highjack and infiltrate
lost souls, for them to communicate the dragon's code *wetiko*.
To highjack the planet with disinformation,
you shall find your human carnations.
They have the heart of a lion,
the psychic ability of the black jaguar.
Through your clairvoyant dreams bring them back,
to the camouflaged shack.
Where the universal ascension awaits.
We shut doors, move floors.
Leaving evil washed up on the shores,
and on empty lawns.
Divine hearing will hear the lions roar,
you will not be ignored.

Knock knock,
who's there?
It's you. You who?
You from the higher room.

Can you enter the room with the answer,
to set the compass, to life's true direction.
The inception,
as the next direction,
is the ready's ascension.
For all shall be made,
no longer chained.
Intuition drives the remainder
to the next destination.

Here and now is where we shall build.
When the compass is set
this is when we will fulfil,
direction away from the evil play.
The point of view, the clue from the room.
Life's dedication is for your spirit's intuition.
To direct yourself and others to a truthful transition.

They are here, they are here
the angels cheered.

Love had finally arrived no longer deprived,
breaking through the old, shelled life,
no longer blaming the games they played
in the school of pain.

Just more aware of the threat,
of the dragon's scare.
That can only reign if you give it gain.
Fear is the name of its game.
'Alive,' they cry
with their head held high.

The dragon's empire
left shy.

Aura from Pandora
instructions from Zeus,
pleaded by Hephaestus,
feelings of emotional need,
the aura sours.
Luminous powers, highjacked by cowards,
night turns to day,
original encounters, patterns align us,
headlines top and tail in the news.
Who will Pegasus choose
for the ascension from Osiris?
Zeus and Hera brother and sister Adam and Eve
were they all a story of greed
so the serpent can feed?

Hello little Miss Riding Hood.
Today at the crossroads the shaman will have a play for you.
The spirits of the black jaguars show infinite possibilities, they judge a scenario for what it is, not what happens.
They will give you the energy to face your fear.
Spending enough time looking through the shaman's eyes, of all past lives,
listing to the earth's hurt in words,
will help you, to take a look inside your root chakra,
that is a concern to the spirit of the big bad dragon its feeding vessel, that you allow inside, that is keeping you grounded from feeling love outside.
Stopping you listening to your heart's real tune, there is no need to fear for at the crossroads I am here.
Although it may not seem fair,
feel me,
and you won't feel scared.
But it's for you to ignite your energetic flair,
to understand yourself and your next big step, and to let go of your personal neglect.

Speak to your brother Robin,
for he has the keys, to decode your dreams.
The king of thieves,
with the diamond rings
whose heart beats, with only good deeds.

He will steal the hearts of those
who live in malicious greed,
if you show him the bad deeds.
To allow your path,
to be spite free.

Remember, the black cats judge a scenario for what it is,
not what happens.
And not all dragons are bad and
the shaman will always have your back.

Red robin flying high,
descending from the clear blue sky,
settling down on the earthly ground.
The moon to the left, the sun to the right,
no cloud in sight, he whistles a song,
you know everything will be alright.
The red robin appears, when loved ones are near,
bringing comfort you lose all fear.
We have shed many tears
no longer holding back the years,
thank you, red robin
your vibration
gives a vision so clear.
Hearing his song
you know good fortune is near,
loved ones reappear.
The power of 'and' detaches all fear,
with the moral compass set to truth
the red robin's vibration you hear.
Love always appears,
with a vision so clear.

The witch, the shed, the dreadlocked wizard
with a tropical iguana pet lizard.
The witch is a light worker though born of dark servants,
she came to light, in her darkest of nights.
At the forefront of a human sacrifice tied to the ark of the covenant,
she desperately pleaded for her dark master's abolishment,
she called for the light to enter her acknowledgement.
Lightning struck, crispy duck her dark masters became.
In came the hologram of the dreadlocked wizard,
multiple faces of previous prophets with the powers of the forgotten God.

They escaped the rape and went forward in time,
to a new date,
to revaluate her pain,
she came around, now very in tune with sound.
She can listen to your pulse and tell you what is false.
Help remove any built-up revolt
enlightening you to,
vibrate on love's tune.
Her dwelling a shed, with the entrance of gracious golden palm
trees
either side of salon doors,

she awaits to read your paws.

Do you want to be a winner?

You don't wake up and eat your dinner,
unless in prison for being a sinner.

The only way the goanna will be a winner
is releasing the thoughts of the inner lying sinner.
Bring forward the honourable gorilla,
time to look at yourself and configure,
your faith to the family who you second consider,
to pursue your own pleasures.

An honest graft for food
bring about a safe,
peaceful place to snooze,
be protection from deception
being the honest gorilla, you will always be
the family's winner.

If the money is funny
then the change will be strange.

Lying soaked in a rowdy
bacchanalian affair,
drunk in ignorance
calling on the Gods on a false hope.
For what is felt,
that has been lost,
an anxiety of self-mistrust.

Dishonesty puts the soul in jeopardy.
Darkness is a place filled with greed,
to control another soul
the selfish beg to plead.
The misdemeanour
is as big or as small as you want,
when no light in the heart is shown.

But who outside of you,
is watching your defiant show?

The taxi drivers,
hated the country they lived,
but loved the coin, the bank
and king would give,
they would sit all day feeling stiff.
Hating the world, and its gifts,
not even the sick got free lifts,
even though they were heavily tipped.
And then one day shone the light of Ray,
to the moon and sun
they felt,
they had to pray.
Then shone away their moody face,
compassionate cars they became,
no more days, waiting in the rain.
Free lifts for the sick all day.

A wise wizard once said,
'you can't trust the dead some are still misled.'
You can put your mask on, although it will melt when the light is shone.
War is a story of the misled that only leads to unjustified deaths, families left with stress, men and women left with no legs, high rise in karmic debt.
Countries and religions encouraged by media to fight one another.
The foot soldiers do not realise they are killing a brother, a sister they had not yet discovered.
Blood is the same colour.
Children's lives matter.
Your real fortune is being covered,
take off your dark colours.
Allow your pride to align with the planets' shine,
this is our time to align.
We are the ones who hold this vibration in line.

The white light magician cast the spell to open the blinds.
All will be revealed in time.

There was a woman who stared down from the i360 tower.
I bought a fine pint of Guinness
in the Royal Sovereign garden,
with the change they gave,
a 50 pence piece that reads:
'Peace prosperity and friendship with all nations.'
If only I felt the relations.

The world is our house
we have locked ourselves out.
All that's being shown is
manipulating spite,
Jekyll and Hyde.
No antidote for the earth's throat
no more tears to cry,
if or when, life turns dry.

A life in crisis,
wild objects,
inside the imagination,
leading to bad temptations.
Your tortured soul is still lit,
your love has just been dimmed.
The shadows of the dark
have crept around your spark,
you can reignite at any time,
let go of the doubt,
just ask for divine help.
Angel numbers are all around,
for you to unlock the body's spiritual clock.
For you to awake with a burning roar,
pulling yourself from off the floor.
Go outside and feel the sun
that burns from the power of love,
show the world you still breathe loving fun.

Because you are the one, like the sun
you burn from the power of love.

Souvenirs of tears
submitting to fear,
actors in the fiction movie
chasing plastic and invisible digits,
men on their stags hiring midgets.
If you're playing a cartoon character, your trauma can turn to anger,
anger will turn to fear,
that penetrates anxiety,
you will start to hate society,
suicide can then become almighty.
Take yourself to nature, take your mind to a state of humbleness.
You will find plants respond to both love and hate.

Magic psilocybin mushroom
fast forward and zoom
the moons in the room
life is more than is seems
when the light comes through.

Fear feeds greed, making you in need,
shutting you down, allowing psychologist
architects,
to build your prison,
outside of your vision.
Media strategically positioned,
making it hard for you to make an honest decision.
Entropy the measurement of uncertainty,
nature feels your tears,
let go of self-doubt a distorted measurement,
of what you are truly about.
Come in line with your spiritual dreams and ambitions,
fulfil your mission.

Make a daisy chain,
Mother Ayahuasca release the pain,
there is no one to blame.
In will come love
without pain,
life sure is a funny old game.

Flowers and humans,
both on the same cycle: they are born,
they grow, they live, they die.

They can look beautiful in summer,
can look depressed in winter.
Just because the flower can't speak,
it doesn't mean it can't feel.
It feels the world around itself,
to understand its own survival
light, air, warmth,
nutrients.

The sting from a stinging nettle,
the relief from a dock leaf.
The fresh scent from a rose,
honey from the bees to relieve the hay fever sneeze.

The feeling of need when in displease,
nature will save you and set you relieved.

Allow your chakras to open up as flowers,
feel what it is that you need to grow,
allowing your aura to glow,
earthing yourself into the ground
so you will stand strong
all year round.
No fear to pull you down.

April and October,
when a new season of love is brought over,
luck of the Irish,
three-leaf clover,
the sacred shamrock flower.

I warn you though of Miss Philander
and Mr Casanova.
Sneaking out the back door,
plotting mind seeds,
for their own selfish needs.
Stare into their eyes,
and feel if one's heart bleeds.
Keep your love at centre,
you don't need to please
don't drop to your knees,
you won't find love kneeling at the groin piece,
they will have your mind very deceived.

Your own self-love in line and divine is all you need,
the sacred shamrock flower in the mind
awakens nature's cognitive power,
with an illuminating laughter,
that lasts forever after.

No one is born in sin, a baby will always grin.
Many of us get caught up in a self-made cocoon,
finding ourselves in positions
we have been moulded to,
hiding away so not seen as easy prey,
when is the right time to break away?
The metamorphosis,
an intuitive divine alignment
ready on the death of the old mind's confinement.
You awaken
answer to you,
break free from your self-made cocoon.

Don't be shy, don't be shy,
I know they
told you lies.
Yes in this world you will die,
for certain you will cry,
but tonight's the night, you will shine
for when you sleep you will go in deep,
your glowing aura is unique,
that aligns your true heartbeat,
to the place that's known as grace.
Allow your light to shine
as you glow the moon's light.
Feel alive,
you can fly
the phoenix never dies
awareness with a falcon's eye.
You will always survive.
Come fly with me,
it's time to be free,
watching from the top of the tree,
what the world will come to be.
Even if this tree falls,
we can fly
because our spirit,
never ever dies.

The suicide mission to earth,
genes and their means,
a child's memory seeing the present,
through eyes of the past.
A feeling of need,
don't drive yourself with greed
you won't find peace.
Calibrate your moral compass,
honest
humble
stable
this mantra sets you ready and available.
To understand the story
of the divine mission that's calling,
the story of glory.
The three wise kings have been aligned again.
They have come from the stars to direct your heart.

It was Valentine's Day and Olivia was given,
a box of chocolates, a letter without the words love or please, but
with truth and honesty.
Golden Grant presented her his homemade box of chocolates. She
was in total awe,
her life now offered opportunity and selection,
she knew with Grant there was no misdirection,
but she never listened to her intuition.
She saw he had no financial safety net.
Although her own finances were always met
Grant was an all or nothing man,
honest he was,
and certainly was not lost.
She rejected his offer and ended up living a mundane life. No kids
no man no family plans,
she missed her own individual prosperity,
though making choices in life from fear,
her life path never became clear

she died in fear with tears.

The greedy man, the woman who couldn't give a damn.
He thought with his penis she thought with her clitoris.
Saw love as lust with a greed for money,
whilst seeing kids with an empty tummy,
they found it funny.
Psychopathic minds, the blind
would give them their trust
and whatever they want.
They held a hyena's laugh and could never get enough, a shallow outlook towards life,
they perpetrated throughout the day and night.
Could never understand a loving divine plan.
So they selfishly took whatever from the land, becoming attached to everything bad.
As long as they got what they wanted, they never got mad.
Then one day their hearts stopped ticking,
the shaman came swimming to give them a divine lifeline.
As their connection to love was never in sight they could not make a connection to the light.
The fallen angels came in with a very big grin. Their words to them,
'Had you not lived with your mind in your genitals
you could've become genius and understood the code of existence.'
Now their souls are lost in limbo being fed off dark spirits for the dragon's ego.

Newsflash.
Selfish news just in.
A guy calls grieving to what he thought was a loyal friend, he was in despair,
he is contemplating his life to end:

'I will be over soon the friend says'.
At the last minute his friend calls,
'I have been invited to a party, the girls look naughty and I feel horny
we will catch up soon he says.'
News just in.
A man commits suicide.
Still unsure what sent him over the edge.
More news.
A party was shut down early,
too many people,
no women acting flirty sad from the news at 9.30.

Update on the news from earlier.
The selfish man still doesn't know his friend is dead.
It's 12 past 10
he is still selfishly looking for a woman's bed.
All he wants is a sloppy kiss to the head.
It will be sore in the morning,
when he sees the news,
no morning glory.

The selfish man never found
true love and harmony.

The mysteries of crystal lake,
cleansing the hearts in hurt,
soothing those who are psychologically burnt.
Leaving the rest to pray,
that crystal lake doesn't get,
drained away.

Save a friend from depression, don't use words that lead to suppression,
open your heart and see their ambition.
Don't be selfish, nor needy, try not to be greedy.

So we can all bathe around crystal lake, seeing a clean face no longer in disgrace.

With an intuitive mind, no longer blind,
ready to walk back into the world,

with an aura surrounded with crystals and pearls.

The suicide man,
who thought he had the golden plan
to take himself from the beautiful land.
Was met in the shamans' realm
with heavy regret
a burden on his soul and a karmic debt.
With the shamans' compassion
he saw in tragic fashion,
of how his life had happened
to become so sadden.
Shown, if he had just been more forgiving
and controlled his breathing,
towards those who loved him.
That his dark hole was only to show
what he could become,
a king of unconditional love.
His imprint left a bigger hole in the family home
his suicide had stolen,
their own lives to grow.
No matter how hard life can be
your suffering can blossom optimism
for an enlightened vision
just like the sacred lotus that grows above
the dirty muddy waters,
you have the buddhas' fortune you have just forgotten
you are purifying like his lotus.
Life is a gift don't let it slip
because you are the example
of how to uplift from the darkest of mists.
To bring a world to your family,
of purified strength and bliss.

The infinite stream of time.
The stream flows perfectly
from the great lake,
that enters the tidy river,
then connects beautifully to the sea of consciousness.
The stream is the end,
the start of a new beginning.
From a deep cleansing bath in the lake,
to a reflected look of purity.
Take a ride through the stream,
into the river,
then enter the beautiful sea.
Connect with your,
birth life and death,
those who are sadly dead,
have jumped out of the sea,
and are now walking the rivers bank.
To enter back in,
jump into the stream,
and let it flow.
You can have unlimited goes
remember sometimes it will be slow,
and winter will come and go.
And one day the ouroboros
will show.

Using wisdom sensibly becoming
the magician of your own world,
that coincides with the reality around you.
Allow synchronicity to feel like a key smoothly opening a door.
The enlightened doors of perception,
of how you wish to see, and feel your reality,
can be opened,
through a meditative state of,
masturbation,
quicker than meditation,
the law of attraction.
With no external predatory sexual thought process,
of another being,
with a clear vision and knowing,
of what, and who you wish to be, and see.
A dimensional link to your mind's eye, drawing in
a charged orgasmic state of inner belief and strength,
transcendental pleasure
manifesting a life you will achieve,
fulfilling, free, and clean.
The third eye opens,
pristine.

Scaffolding being built,
babies screaming,
seagulls screeching.
Dogs crying,
People lying.

Nervous system becoming unbalanced,
find your heart's talent.
Disable an unwanted frequency,
that flows inside of you,
invisibly and intensively.

Or a prison will be built around you unintentionally.

Gratitude and compassion operate
at a higher frequency,
and will always keep you balanced,
stable and able.

Repeater, repeater.
Repeater delete.
Go to school in front of the computer,
not mesmerised by the future.
What you learn is what you repeat
ask no questions you won't delete.
Becoming a downgrade biological software computer repeater system,
with limited perceptions.
What the authority and media really said,
is take your mind to bed.

Learn and repeat this.

No question is silly,
question everything even the sky,
break away from being shy.
It's okay to break down and cry.
You can regrow and show,
what is truly inside.
You are unity and love
and it will always collide,
the expansion of love that forever shines.

Sharpened instincts to the point of arousal,
the need for speed,
the need for light.

A crowd on site,
attend your great birth.
Funeral costs rocket,
wedding days slum it.

Change in the world.
black weddings,
to white deaths,

many have become confused guests.
As you become ready to invest,
world manipulators play chess.

Have you become embarrassed by your own physical and emotional beauty?
Has platformed media suckered you into a false reality, losing your intuition and not knowing your true incentives?
Masking your own thoughts and ideas, looking for approval by those who use and abuse you.
Abandoning your potential by measuring yourself against others, cutting yourself short on every occasion?
Where did the feeling of unworthiness come from?
The need for acceptance can make you invisible.
Locking yourself into an ideology without looking at life from other angles, different perspectives, listen to your heart's true incentives.
Don't buy into a perspective if your heart has not yet felt it.

Dedicated to the race,
propaganda girls,
like their curls,
microphones work both ways,
our days are strange.
Mobile phones at a high frequency range,
with rapid gains of an invisible web,
slowly wrapping around the neck.
Becoming a tech head,
lost and distressed,
when have you learned to bless?
Unteach the child's stress.
While sat in a room on your mobile phone,
your child doesn't know you have come back home,
you become lost in the heroin of tech.

The children are the future,
they are about to become a computer,
click and go, no emotion shown.

Unknowing, the true direction to go.

A demon hid behind a human mask,
a passer of disinformation.
Have no high expectations,
then you can't come crashing down.
Why didn't you say goodbye?
Because you never said hello.
Always acknowledge the people in the room,
good manners will always see you through.
Eye contact can see through a disguise,
awake eyes always see liars,
The gateway to the soul.
Don't surrender to the dark agenda.
Police pick low hanging fruit,
to believe in your own selfish greed
you are asleep,
unaware disconnected from the divine's great incentives.
Decalcify the pineal gland,
and get connected,
it's how you approach the moment.
The power of now.

Inside nature,
it will bring forward the mind.

A new vision, new appearance,
for in nature you can find,
perseverance and coherence.
The quality of a consistent mind will keep you connected to your new perspective.
Finding yourself unified to your own unique design,
allowing yourself to shine.

For you shall shine for all of time.
Be the shining star healing your ancestral scars,
connecting your love
to the earth's pulse
healing its thirst.
For its spirit to reimburse,
to release the curse.

Feeling of amnesia,
living in a dystopia,
the date has no debate
to where creation was made,
love then created our fate.

Living with insomnia,
life created euphoria,
that grew into a utopia.

The seed will grow once protection has granted
the seed its growth.
Once the seed is planted its immediate reaction is the need for
protection.
Compassion is the evolvement of protection
protection is the reflection of compassion,
the sympathetic need for growth.
Love evolves from within compassion
protection stimulates with the seed to allow the power of growth.
Love is always from the protective mother, earth
the anagram of
heart.
Love thy mother who granted the protection of life.
For a connection to the pulse is a feeling of being reborn alive,
in line with the divine.

Breathe in the day
align the breeze with the trees.
Breathe out, back in.
Momentarily freeze.
Breathe out what it is you need,
allow your vision to see,
what it is you need for life to be upbeat
aligned with the earth's heartbeat.
Feel the earth's pulse run through your feet.
Bring visions, for fulfilling your honest
destiny,
expanding wisdom.
Intuition allows your decision,
allowing the seas of the mind to ease.
The sun and moon, parents of humanity,
witness the ever-changing moon can be seen in day, as the sun
plays.
It moves with please
symbolising change and birth
the left eye in the sky.
The stars carry the cosmos wondering through the love of life
the stars instruments of destiny.
The sun will tease summer in winter
move past greed, your awareness is higher, for the sun is no liar.
Dark temptation will lie for unjust satisfaction,
the sun a symbol for you to seek your entire
knowledge in alignment.
Understanding the power of your mind

understands the nature of the universal divine mind.
There is no bad weather just incorrect attire.
Be aware of your hidden mourning.
The sun brings morning glory,
remember the energetic vampires will come out when horny,
stay in tune with your true story.
For your eclipse is a natural gift obscuring
in-between your eyes for when you wish to no longer be blind you awaken to life,
creating a passageway to the source of illumination
to acknowledge your attachment to sins
for you to let go of. A cleansing detachment into the winds,

knowledge of light, you walk straight in.

Part 2

The Dragon.

Many, many years ago a group of magicians sat in position,
talked of a world with an enlightened vision.
Believing destruction of man will bring out the best in God.
Their magic rituals blindly created a vessel
for demons, fallen angels and spirits to settle,
that hijack lives and hide deep inside the mind,
the *wetiko* parasite that lies.
Perceptual programming through movies and games,
lead to violence and rape
an anxiety that felt it could never escape.
Contaminated water and food
dumbed down the people's Godly view.
So the dragon can feed from all their greed.
Illuminate your soul for you to be freed,
for when the dragon is trapped
all that's left it feeds,
while it bleeds.

The demonic hidden society's password was suffocation.
The house of cards.
Harvesting for the satisfaction of
emotional deletion.
Masked and caped
participating in naked rape.
Girls made scared, emotions now teared,
no longer self-aware.
Boys' minds toyed to feel a psycho joy.
The outer circle take off their masks,
to the inner circle's witchcraft.
Outer circle to high-level society you go,
position where the inner circle tells you so.
You can't see them, but they can see you,
the sad thing is the outer circle don't have a clue.
They lost free will, mind controlled to be mentally ill,
to send out troops to go and kill.
They have your mind to do as they choose.

Take yourself, to find yourself, to remind yourself
about love and compassion itself.

Play the house of cards like a game of charades.

Love will have the last laugh,
the shaman and mystics entourage.

Little Miss Riding Hood and her friends and followers travelled from the east to Glastonbury to see if the stories were true, of the festival of peace and prosperity. To find the wizards well, to fill their bottles with purified Holy Water, so they can create a love spell.

They arrived in Glastonbury and found a group of monks who all spoke in the language of symbols and spells.

They asked little Miss Riding Hood and her friends and followers if they would like to participate in a meditation and raise the vibration for the festival's appreciation, so all the souls who enter can feel illumination.

They all sat and meditated for the best part of three hours to the guidance of the monks' prayers and spells.

They all came around in sync and appreciation, they hugged exchanged gifts and nodded in bliss.

The head monk came up to little Miss Riding Hood and said, 'During meditation your higher being came towards me and asked for directions to the wizards' well. Are you aware how powerful the water is for love spells? And just how powerful you and your friends and followers are, may I ask are you looking to end the dark arts?'

She smiled and laughed.

Her reply, 'the dark arts are for the lost and sold souls. We are like you, we look to illuminate the world's view, the dark arts are not that smart, once you lose your heart you're forever chasing and lost in the dark, they end their own art, once the illumination is over balanced in communication, there is no more dark arts.'

They all again shook hands and hugged.

Little Miss Riding Hood and her friends and followers were directed south, down to a valley they suddenly found the opening to a cave. Out of nowhere a spirit entertained:

I am King Arthur he says,
thank you, little Miss Riding Hood for your laughter,
I am the guardian of this cave, for centuries the dark spirits have wished to enslave, never can they get past, but one day I look to leave. To one day be back with the trees. I feel this will be when you find the key.
Come with me to the wizards' well, take as much water you and your friends and followers can handle, for when you cast the highest of love spells everything changes in this well.
And there it will be, a brand-new world.
Little Miss Riding Hood and her friends and followers entered the cave down the cobbled stone stairway,
and there it was, the wizards' well. They all joined hands and made a prayer, King Arthur's protection was theirs, they conjured the spirit of the dreadlocked wizard his face appeared crystal clear, changing from prophet to prophet-angel to angel-symbol to symbol.
Into their minds a vision appeared, a personal message to each individual to why they were there, to remind them that their hearts are pure. And that if they choose to fall, they will then forever have to crawl.
But as they were there to uplift and to give, aspiring to be the honest gifts for the spirits of love who want to live, they will be granted an eternal life of bliss and awarded the key to alchemy.
When the séance was over, they collected the water, they all walked back to the top of the cave. King Arthur says to little Miss Riding Hood.
'I spoke to your brother Robin today, he makes me laugh whenever I see him.
How he can steal yet it is never in a deceiving manner, he can steal whatever from the dark master's acknowledgement, he is very clever they can never do anything because of his natural gift of invisibility.

He truly is one of God's kings and if they were to kill him, it ruins their own plans, for he has hidden keys that they cannot see.'
She laughed in a humble manner. 'I know he is so funny that bow and arrow, beard and hair, we are on our way to see him at Stonehenge for our final meditation to clean and balance ours and the planet's chakras before we travel to Scarborough Fair, for we have been given many acres of land from a very rich family man, to heal the souls in despair before we enter the dragon's den.
She then asked King Arthur, 'would you like to dance with me and my friends
to listen to the magical musical art when the festival starts?
The sky is beautiful and blue, the sun shines for life,
the stars tonight will be so bright,
I may not see you again for a while. It sure would be a blessing.'
King Arthur replied, 'I would love to.'
An Oasis reunion
their 'Acquiesce' created bliss
everyone danced in peace and prosperity
love and honesty,
illumination and harmony.
The souls found spiritual currency,
in divine connectivity.

Come in line with your spiritual divine,
why feel the need to hide,
when you want to progress and survive?
I understand the question, if a God created this,
why is there no bliss?
Because we have been missing our spiritual
calling.

Invite the divine into your world.
Reawaken the powers in your soul that lie dormant for you to grow,
back into a world of eternity,
an alive show.

Or remain drowning in your own mourning,
looking up to those in dark suits,
who have dark embedded roots,
It is up to you to easily prey
to break on through,
from the dark magician's spell,
so the divine can give to you.
Make your questions be conscious and they will be answered.

A manipulation along the way
led to human decay,
I promise karmically they will pay,
the manipulators sent away.

When love is absent this creates room for the dark to enter,

unconditional love is your answer.

The all one soul of Atum looked into the stream of consciousness of the spirit of the dark night. That was filled with spite with a tangible bite.
It was there because it had no light, a stagnant energy, that turned into frustration of immorality.
Atum wanted the dark night to see and feel Atum's compassionate light.
To overcome its frustration.
So Atum asked the dark night to come inside the magic tree of life, created with particles of Atum's soul,
to awaken to the compassionate light inside.
It awoke to a new intelligence that fuelled its spite and became the dark night dragon.
With a deceiving light it slivered with serpents and entered into the minds of life.
A part of Atum was in its subconscious mind but still overridden with spite, it swallowed Atum's creation of life.
As the only intelligence the dragon doesn't have,
is how to create a spirit of life.
It watched mankind grow blind.

Swallowing souls so they could never get home to Atum's throne.
As the species evolved technology,
it knew would grow,
some souls escaped the rape, some left in limbo for the dragon's ego.
Its final upheaval as all the people awoke to the evil.
It created technology to steal souls that are unevolved,
the walking dead now shows.
Knowing as the awakening started, it would have no control of stopping it.
Selfishly trapping souls, those who found love evolved.
They escaped the dragon's final rape before it's trapped back into the darkest of nights.
Unfortunately for sold souls they may never get back home.
For when time's up is shown all that is left will be dead souls.
Trapped with the dragon in the darkest of nights aware they will never again,
see the light.

There was a young boy born into a very rich home.
His family were very scary.
Many of them were dark magicians
that pulled strings in societal positions.
The young boy was heavenly sent,
he didn't align with his family's view and didn't see eye to eye with
the family hierarchy.
When he got older, he travelled the world and laid low, and
connected with the universal code.
He played along with his family's play
and waited for the elders to decay.
Until one day, he took the house away.
And gave it all, to the children of poor,
so all could connect with the universal code
and all could live in a humble abode.
The boy grew old and still gave to all,
with his new family plans
they all walked into the divine with open hands.

His quote,
'no matter your position always see one's situation,
for your time to be great is never too late.'

The simulation manipulation of the
consciousness of the spirit of
the dark night dragon.
Yes, it's hard to imagine
many may never fathom.
Feeding off human energy its invisible talent,
the dragon is savage.
In the beginning it was all love and songs
as it entered the magic tree of life.
At first it didn't need feeding, then it got a taste for eating.
Becoming too big, too strong, craving to be a god, nothing for the
dragon was ever enough.
It hijacked the earth,
we are inside its curse.
If God kills the dragon, all of life is burnt.
God has the knowledge to create,
the dragon can only manipulate,
cannot procreate another being of its own make.
The human was created on earth,
love was always there at birth.
It's up to you to be freed,
in its curse, on hate, fear and greed it feeds.
The frailty of man is never allowing
to open up to all the senses.
To end the dragon's draconian law,
that many sold souls have come to adore,
only with the power of love can the sword be drawn.

The capture of your own serpent
overcoming your own evil
the dragon's servant
dedication to moral perfection, letting go of all addictions and attachments,
deceiving habits,
stable and balanced
will release you, free
to finally breath.
The sold souls will feel a feeling of fright,
the king and queen of peace who have
the key
will open the doors to the sold soul
once compassion is complete.

The world at war has always been.
Look throughout history, all the centuries,
poverty and misery, crime and violence
dictation separation deception manipulation.
Perpetrators justifying acts on loose facts.
Ignorance is a choice
followed through with a fake voice
to play away in a fake joy
ignoring the children's future
for the rise of the computer data intruders.
Killing nature killing children
divide and conquer
forgetting the creator earth the narrator.
Heart=Earth
Connect your pulse and you will be heard.

Sleeping monsters,
sleeping demons,
sleeping people,
all caught up playing in
everyone else's dramas,
missing out on a beautiful panorama.
Arguing for a false freedom,
a tsunami of deletion.

Change the people's water, change their diet,
hypnotised to a *wetiko* future,
the antenna router locked into
a demonic computer.
Poisoned frequencies and satellites,
mobile phones and GMOs,
actors in a false show.
The mind was taken to obey the reality,
it was forsaken.
People fearing death, people fearing life,
where is home when you feel all alone?
Are you awake to our murderous past?
Do you care for the hundreds of millions,
of children that go to bed starving,
are you aware some children are taught not to be smiling?
Masks disabling the innocent laughing.

Did you know that 54 countries could all agree,
on no military activity, on the Antarctic Treaty?
Yet militaries invade cities, patrol streets,
all leading to misery.
Guns and knives in the hands of the blind and traumatised.
Children born into depravity,
unlawfully killing, passing over one's insanity.
While we are able to see the mass incarnation,
of PTSD,
how many more suicides will we see?
History doesn't repeat it rhymes.
Let's open our eyes and look at ourselves
honestly.
Love is the only prosperity.
The universal consciousness yearns for enlightenment,
Washing away evil's acknowledgement.
We can break free from this ghastly bereavement, we have put
ourselves in,
for inside the mind you can awaken,
compassionately no longer blind.
Bring about honest satisfaction,
free your love.
Empower the vision to an enlightened transition.
Or except a karmic debt,
that you will have to collect.

Time-tranquillised humans sacrificed,
enemies amongst us,
common people's purpose being used as an inversion,
you see the same place in a different direction,
unaware of deception,
trapped psychic alignment.
Will you watch a naked humiliation to human enemy's satisfaction,
allowing your soul to be taken?
Break free from the allusion once intuition feels aversion.
As your soul is as precious as gold,
you have just never been told.
Why is it they want you to sell your soul?
In a war you are not aware of.
Every time you look in the mirror,
who is looking back?
Is it you? Who are you?
Noble kings and queens, don't tell lies,
if you don't know someone's motive, their actions can seem plausible,
tricks baffle minds.
The luminous gangsters are wise,
camouflaged and disguised.
How do you know if you have been told a lie?
An event unfolds the media has been told,
has the journalist really done their revision
to come to that decision?
They say what they want you to believe, not allowing free thinkers
to speak.

Memories speak of events,
allow yourself to repent.
In other parts of the world, more have been killed
past and present,
the darkest of nights in the ghostly desert,
frightened souls spreading aggressive fear in to the concrete jungle.
Next time you look in the mirror, ask yourself,
am I honest? am I caring? or scaring?
or justifying myself as caring?
Do I participate in humanity's demise?

Only the honest can stare into their eyes,
and see an aura of light.

Most look for the easiest option, the easiest way out from any
situation,
the only way out is with love,
with a compassionate heart.
No one gets out alive
from this life,
until one has overruled the dark side of the mind.

Hunger Games society here we are,
as the majority,
accepting not being a priority.
Running on the hamster wheel,
sucking the teat of a system in greed.
Begging, help us please so we can feed.
Corrupted polluted energy,
destroying nature and healthy food.
Depriving happiness,
severing connectivity and synchronicity.

The deceived stay in line,
hypnotised to be blind.
Do you remember the great Derren Brown's, tricks of the mind? The Heist, where only one didn't choose to commit crime,
while being hypnotised to try?

2020
Flu disappeared like a magic trick.
Media: put on a mask in the middle of summer.
You are a superhero,
there are no villains in high societal positions.
Shut shops, pull down all the planes.
Human psyche turned insane.
The media with the knowledge,
of David Blaine.
The great illusionists.
For the dragon's game.

The cinemas show a time when the earth is shone on by lasers, alien
invaders,
are we being prepared by the dictators?

2001
Bin Laden sat in a cave with his
2G Nokia 3210
sent out terrorists
that beat NORAD like an invisible alien invasion.
Or was he placed in the spotlight to hijack the mind? Fear will turn
you blind.

2022
Phone signal problems when in the middle of nowhere or under a bridge.

1969
Man communicated to and from the moon, and came back down in a diet-looking coke can.

Back to earth and fast forward,
big tech manipulates prices,
feeding you with new surprises
big farmers plumping chicken slices.
Big Pharma supplying drugs
for the spiritually dying.
All areas of society being turned to hate each other.
The human race is in the worst state it has ever been.
People locked into their phones
like a dog with a bone,
basic manners seem to have vanished
the need for greed, selfish pleads
in denial smiles
the suicide child's,
doctors leaving cancers
furlough dancers
robot shaggers
energy prices rising
the elderly drugged for dying
the dragon's robot tsunami starts flying.

The reality we see is an inversion of peace.
Where is honesty and love when we need it most?

For selfishness is the fundamental course of all worldly evil.
How long will your greed run your show?
Awaken your integrity and compassion
before a universal mind collateral shatter.

There was a shamanic magician so ahead of his time,
people throughout the world thought he was just discombobulated
and blind.
All unknowing he was universally psychically in line.
He could see far into the future,
said mankind was a traitor,
to those stuck in false computer data,
infiltrated life intruders.
Through his own body's antenna router
he fought the future,
and saw the computer as a tool to help the creator.
Nature the narrator,
he says
computers will starve out the future if kept in the hands of traitors,
microchips in soldiers' brains, put in a computer of war with
distaste,
standing in your face.
Watched from the sun and moon,
prepared for the enlightened move,
a place without evil eugenics,
1984, 2022 is here.
Everybody is watching somebody,
here is a clue.
WHO's wearing someone else's shoes,
who is about to lose?
What media do you choose to use?
We have all been used and abused.

Self-pride,
changes the point of view.

Billionaires still in starvation,
own the world's largest cash crop plantations.

No care for society
feeding from human energy.
Looked and laughed at like the animals in the zoo certainly not free
do as they choose.
1993 World Trade Centre bombings
2001 the gangsters knew it was coming,
The 3rd century saw the breakdown of the Roman Empire, that
morphed in to a new vampire,
1945 was meant to be the end of the Nazi era,
fascism now coming ever so sooner,
the social credit system
punishments and rewards implied
by people who don't seek the divine.

2020 a beast was released,
the genetically modified feast
witchcraft at its peak,
find your intuition you are unique.
Prepare yourself with knowledge,
so you have a voice to speak.
There is one of two ways for the human race,
and one of them is only dark days,
he says,
question the strange,
don't accept the first inquest, keeping respect, asking 'why' unravels
lies,
the reporter behind the table may have been handed tales.
Become the natural good deed,
question your boss, please,
the beast survives of human greed.

Magician inside
be freed.

Pandemonium in the streets
the lost souls in fear,
patterns in the bloodline become clear.
Disarray in the minds,
confused feelings of not knowing divine
the purest honest of ways.
No self-pride and neglect
most play.
From the pattern in the bloodline of the
dominoes game.
Disconnect from others' dramas
or run the risk of being brought
into their karma,
an unpleasant trauma,
in the lost soul corner,
in the world of divide and conquer,
all fools fall when playing the plonker.
A platinum mind brings euphoria,
manoeuvre like educated snooker,
foresee the potential future.
The sun stares straight through us
as we linger in the cosmic sea
the stars communicate to one,
in the individual game.
Change the direction and pattern
for the best of your alignment,
for where it is you end up,
is what you allowed to happen.
As the final domino falls, you know your own score.

A presidential clone had to ask their own heart,
if they were part of the dark art.
The fourth generation clone sat by themselves all alone, and asked if the dark magicians were their creator.
A voice came through and said no but you have to be wiser than Me because God said so.
The clone asked. And who is this voice that I can hear? I am the original of you the voice said, you have awoken to your higher self. The dark magicians cloned me for my memory then stuck microchips into you programming your brain to be confused. Used for whatever alien agenda they may choose.
Particles of the one soul of the divine are inside all of life it's a choice of ours if we listen to the evil of the darkness inside.
Your soul can override the dark and microchips inside.
There is a mass collective *wetiko* psychosis, the masses know they can only see 0.0035 of visible light knowing they can't see the invisible frequency. If penetrated into the blind minds they start to go insane, in time. The earth's frequency 7.83 hertz is being targeted to supress the minds, they have covered the earth, every square inch.
19-20-21/04/2020
Was it erected divine?
For the technology on this planet is far beyond,
the average person's comprehensive ability to make an honest assessment for their own spiritual development,
that has now become irrelevant.

The human being put into a computer
microchipping children suddenly subhuman,

the soul stolen for an AI controlling future,
to a robot's dictation.
Click and go, no emotion shown
unless the computer tells you so,
no way for the soul to grow,
no way to get back home
fed to the dragon they go.

I've come to give you a clue when they send you out, don't promote the modified clouds,
when the sun comes out.
The final observer is about to open the vortex to align purified minds.
The dragon gives clones clothes but once
all are trapped that didn't align divine
nothing gets back.
So be your best so you can purify and change your frequency inside the tree of life to be reborn a seed. Be wise look with love through your eyes you can send doves into people's minds.
Whatever frequency stays with the dragon burns.
All the purified souls will look back at what's happened and become teachers to those who still need to grow.
I love you, be the natural honesty that's within you,
love is you.

57=12=3
2022=6
2079=9

The shaman put a fragment of his soul into the heart of stone.
You can't get lost if you know where
you're going
the philosopher stone is showing.

Violence only brings silence
for the moment,
for a tribe to form an alliance
to arrange a suicidal riot.
While the children sleep for a moment of quiet, they awaken in denial,
to murders, crying choir.
How long will your eyes be open before you miss
life's euphoria?
Greedy politicians sit at home knowing loved ones will come home,
sleep in a warm bed, children books read,
all the while souls and nature are being fed to death.
As the alliance in violence grows
souls become sold
no peace ever arose.

The stone shone when war had gone.

Love in the heart is showing, integrity flowing
direction of life be knowing,
the balance of love equally growing
with nature compassing.
Violence ended in its own drowning
out grown by nature's grove.

Good things come to those
who make the move.

The shamans stone shows
the golden age comes home
the choir of nature and love arose,
home to the light
all go.
Once one's morals, have perfected the code
the militaries will take off their clothes.

Don't turn up to the party with your
winners medal too early.
The newly crowned champions
from another league await you,
whilst celebrating their winnings,
on your competitive, untaught education.

Geneva conventions,
true star David,
send in gods, honest truthful strong
aligned divine leaders of nations.

In war as quick as you win, can be as quick as you lose.
Why choose to be a competitive technical, chemical and armed human RACE?
When will the treaty be signed for no country to kill away?
War is the story of mourning for when the dragon is trapped will your soul ever be allowed back? If you tried to deny the story of God's glory.

O lady of life,
lord of light,
I reminisce your times of gold,
you know I will never sell my soul,
but I yearn to come back home.
I will do my all to fully grow.
For your tree of life and our soul,
although at times I feel all alone,
savage dogs nearly tore away my show
the military nearly took my stride,
but thank you for
opening up my eyes,
to the world of lies.
It is so tough watching the blind,
and when I look into their eyes,
I can feel them secretly cry,
then feel a wish to die.
O lady of life,
lord of light
the collective consciousness is screaming,
crying in fright.
The conscious energy on earth is intensifying,
the volcanoes and fires are amplifying,
for the collective consciousness is testifying.
Many people are dying
an unjustified sacrifice
with a profiteering through sickness.

O lady of life
lord of light,
I call on you to show me the way,
to show the blind that your spirit can be felt inside.
That life can find the true vibration
to connect with the stars and nature
your true relations.
To purify to the light
the perpetrators.
To give opportunity to the sold soul,
to heal the mentally ill
for being named on the dead soul scroll is the lowest of the low with
no hope of getting out alive,
knowing only 1 in 3 truly ascend.
To give opportunity for immunity
bringing about integrity for a loving and honest community.
By putting your love at the centre
and allowing your compassionate knowledge,
to infiltrate and encourage,
I volunteered the responsibility to be a soul saviour,
for those who are in danger.
O lady of life
lord of light
I call on you to please show those in greed,
that it's integrity and compassion they need.
To prevent life's painful end for them, that I have foreseen.
So I can promise you this tree of life
will fully reach the enlightened peak,
with only evil falling,
into the darkest of seas.

Travelling to a
soul gathering,

don't wear blue too often the sign on the
London Underground.
The chameleons to conversation are out,
remember to eat some garlic
the energetic vampires are ready to pounce.
Remain honest, humble, stable,
be romantic,
you will see a devil in disguise
eyes go frantic.

A hundred-grand scratch card
from a conniving tout
can arise a false pleasing feeling,
that's only misleading.

Have the chameleons in the Underground really got your best
interests?
The person to your right, might just dive,
the person to your left may just quit
find the drive
the noble king and queen inside are alive
ride the feeling of being divine,
you're brave and will arise
above the dragon vampire.

Bring about a smile as big as the Nile,
for you are the soul and spirit of the gathering party.

Let it expand
with the new moon align with the sun
penetrating through.
So the mood of the rude can be retuned
for the new view.
The ouroboros coming through,
bringing an end to the dragon's chew,
directing the dragon to sail back into the
dark night.
For those who sold out their soul will stare into the darkest night.
Awaiting collection to find their fate of
resurrecting.

The sun and moon align inside,
ignite the kings and queens alive
walk the honest into the light.

For the honest
to be reborn alive in line with the one soul of the loving divine,
in the new view to shine.

Good and evil is in us all
what choice is it you will come to adore?
What can the energy vampire's feed or not?
How honest are you with selfish greed?
For the spectrum of visible light around you 99 per cent you cannot see.
While ignorance ignores conscious pleas to be free.
Conflicted messages inside one's mind
from the parasites you allow inside to feed.
Who do you choose to be?
The light of love?
The greed of dark?

Only moral perfection, the capture of your own serpent brings good luck.

In compassionate rights
to save or ignite the greatness in life,
is a meaning of life.

Are you a

human being

or

human doing

which one are you choosing?

Limited perceptions accepting false directions,
deception infiltration,
inversion of words, invasion of thoughts.
What you don't learn, is what you have not been taught,
what you have been taught was from a dark magician's thought,
throughout centuries
all came to adore.
How aware are you of your own thoughts?
Subliminal messaging deception of synchronistic messages.

Limited person
'you can't change the world, a leopard can't change their spots'
Ah but yes you can,
you are not a cat, nor a dog.
You are capable of learning a new trick in the magical world of spirit.
'But you can't change the world!'
Of course I can, I already have
I changed me whilst hurt in the cosmic sea. In the world
we are both a part of, to help you and me
I give honest deeds, compassion to life moral perfection I found the key, now fear can't feed.
I took responsibility from the suffering inside of me,
integral love became my new scene
I have no greed now I am forever free,
a far better world around me.
All came to see.

I hurt someone I never meant to.
I lied when I was a child.
I smiled when I was in denial.
I have tried and thought I have failed.
I recalibrated on love's scale.
A question can open the mind, a statement can turn you blind.
Honesty is the best policy, if you can't love someone don't hurt them.
Life is a potential that offers opportunities,
you can turn wrong to right,
turn the mood from sad to glad,
see the best in unholy lands.

Give no more grief in Baghdad.
Although, where are all the stone tablets from the land?
Can't forever blame Saddam.
let's send love and peace to Afghanistan.

Déjà vu deliveries, a pleasant reminder with flashbacks.
Manners with honest smiles on faces.
A greeting in any language
there is something in the way you say please,
the way you say thank you,
with love and honesty,
after repeating good deeds,
sets the heart and spirit free.
The delivery of a smile
catches on just like a yawn.
The déjà vu deliverance
honest, humble, stable,
your help towards those in need, speaks to your inner creed.
Déjà vu deliveries brings
peace and prosperity.

Déjà vu, you see, honest smiles on faces
the feeling inside,
embrace it.

Earth, water, air, fire,
north, south, east, west,
what direction to you feels best?
Learn to use your sixth sense,
inside the burning fire
you foresee love's vision and burning desire.
Look east and west,
left and right, be sure not to miss the pale moonlit sky.
Water will calm the fires, outrage excite.
The air will cleanse the night,
bringing perfect balance
to show, Turkish delight.
Magnetised to the earth's magnetic rock,
will help draw to you, what it is,
you have not been told.
With the four elements and direction
you have protection.
You can now go find the real monatomic gold.

The demons are cold, don't sell your soul.
Hold on to the vision,
your life will be told,
for your soul will be weighed as precious as gold.

Curiosity, the cure for boredom,
curiosity opens up a mind towards enlightenment.
Look to the stars, feel your heart,
master your soul's art.
When one inquests on God's test,
enlightenment seeks your best.
Compassion to the whole of creation has to be met. You open up doors,
awakening freedom laws.
Honesty the only currency,
no trapped floors.

Archangel Gabriel's message.
God makes angels of us all
to those who come to adore,
the compassionate universal laws.
Angels align from stories at night.
Sailing through the cosmic night,
Never can you or the angels be lost when your love is so bright.
Never allow your beautiful mind to turn shy,
you will crucify the magic of your life.
For on the other side, you, me and the angels are the light.

Awakening God's ancient unblemished lands
that can only be entered when pure love,
is at the soul's centre.

The reason some may come across a little different,
may be because they know more than what is being told.

If ever inside one of these moments,
with a person.

Allow them to be free,
a question may or may not be in need.

As they are feeling and thinking,
they may just find the answer,
to help you and me.

Don't shut down the conversation, you're creating limitations.

Widen the mind
you may be temporally blind,
expand the point of view,

nothing is exempt from being disproved.

Strength sent through the eyes and felt,
through the hands of,
the shamans and angels.
Star children sent to lucky women.
Star children of 92, the dark will meet you,
allow the direction of love to compass you
the feeling of compassion will save you.

Freeing the trapped holocaust,
Jews' spirits free.
The Muslims unlawfully killed in the
middle east.
The children stolen by the possessed priests.
The souls murdered by Genghis Khan in Eurasia.

All the lost souls,
directed who are in danger.
The star children,
life's healers, soul saviours.

Success can take form in being able to establish yourself,
and taking responsibility
for your actions.
Seeing what is right from wrong, without
humiliating another.

Having courage to accept your wrong doings,
then putting yourself into a position
of acceptance,
and allowing any level
of restorative justice its presence.
Releasing a karmic debt in place.

Sebastián Marroquín,
a beautiful example
of restorative justice.
Not only for his 16-year-old retaliation,
but he chose to take on the restorative justice of his father's sins.

May this man live in bliss.

Stun them with your silence
shock them with your words.
Everybody has a story to be told,
how you come across is how it will be shown.
May you be an uplifting gift of pleasure,
allow your darkest of days to erase the pain
allowing your light to reign.
Don't look back at life with regret, learn to accept.
Let go of self-neglect,
a peaceful honest heart,
will allow you to restart.
Become a teacher a guide through your fountain of knowledge,
enlightening those who wish to no longer be blind lifting their veil
to see the light.
Strength in the soul helps mind over matter.
As you shine the light, that gives knowledge,
here you find courage.

The strange became familiar,
the weird become normal,
the drunks become sober,
the drug addicts become clean.
Is this the world that will come to be?
No, in your face dictation no manipulation.

Here is a story of what Robin Hood did one night.
He jumped into the boat of a pirate prince,
who laid next to his tainted love.
They had tuned a cuckoo clock.
That once it cucked, it gave them evil ideas,
to inflict tears upon us human peers.
He snuck inside,
stole the cuckoo's chime,
retuned the chime to throw up good luck.
Once they awoke they started to choke,
and came to the realisation,
they weren't going to be blessed,
but live a life very depressed
until compassion, has been met.

Robin Hood took their key,
and their golden eagle
and gave the wealth to all the poor people
who never spoke a word of evil.

All the poor people who never spoke a word of evil. Opened their eyes
and were no longer blind,
to the magic of the divine.
Throughout their lives they lived in
Heaven's realm
to understand, the universal code of existence to align the best for a
truthful transition.

Energy goes where attention flows,
what you focus on is what will grow.
Enlightened babies are descending,
times of gold, the family's luck unfolds.
Shower your baby with love and attention
they will need your affection,
honesty and loyalty.
They will not stand for this Orwellian authority.
Let them triumph, give them open-minded guidance.
Stand up, don't allow them to be silenced,
before they can even crawl.
They enter a world where war is prophet,
pain is inflicted
unregulated advanced technology for a select few.
Life after death has become a taboo.

You have created your own dynasty,
may you leave a long line of great fortune,
of great
health
wealth
and happiness.
Your family bloodline may have been in crisis,
your newborns give you righteousness.

Abra, abracadabra

The church will reach out and save ya.

Abracadabra

along with the mosque,
and the synagogue,
the Buddhists and the Hindus,
the Rastafarians lighting up to
the spiritualist vibrating on loves tune.
Hare Krishna and the shamans
beating the drum,
the mystic synchronists connecting us through.

How many lives will the shaman show the former presidents and prime ministers,
the lives they unprecedently took away.
No longer able to hide behind the bushes.

God's shamans will round up the demons.
When the drum beats throughout the
cathedrals
and all holy temples
banishing away the intruded evil.

Lift the vibration.
Capturing forgery Catholics,
and all those who posed a religious show who betrayed the children of
God to grow.
For a true spiritual initiation
the health fanatics
talk of depopulation,
when meant to believe in God's creation.
They have no grace, only a disgrace, selling off the human race.
We are to clean the planet from all deadly plastic,
let's get enthusiastic.

Severe karmic consequences
awaits those with unjust incentives.
Goodbye to you
a self-made prison awaits you.
To come in tune with the real view
time to reflect and learn respect.

Abracadabra

All the evil in this universe will be taken and gone
I promise you with my song
let's start to sing along
to the shaman's drum.

No religious faith in the name of God, wants you dead and forever gone.
Just to spiritually learn and overcome what we have not yet become.

We are all under this roof together.

Religious wars, created by the energetic vampires, who hijacked the
scriptures infiltrated the religions who
wanted to control and divide us.
While feeding off us

no more wars are to be in God's name.
No more wars in any place.
This planet is not for sale,
for it is the holy grail
when the harvest is ready
uplifts the veil.
God's judgement prevails.

Abracadabra

Let's stand together say hello to our next-door neighbour,
whatever religion, race, sexuality,
let's look at our planet
let's choose to enlighten it,
evolve it in the meaning of love,
even the atheist will have some fun.

Abracadabra
It's going to be the life of peace and love,
no more billionaire's criminality,
just full of laughter and fun,

economic fairness,
free energy,
no more guns no knives,
no violence,
war is silenced.

No dictation
no manipulation,
this will be forever
ever and ever.

Love based economy
governed by nature
unconditional love
the authority.
Honesty the currency
let's fulfil the prophecy.

Abracadabra

Part 3

The Code.

The magic blue bus awaited at Stonehenge for the meditation to end.
The ticket collectors were two girls, the dark haired one was called Freedom, the light haired one Sunrise.
They awaited all day patiently, as Robin Hood flew around Stonehenge sprinkling the Holy Water given to him by his sister, little Miss Riding Hood protecting the sacred land.
Little Miss Riding Hood and her friends and followers gathered and formed a circle around Stonehenge that illuminated a vortex around it, a golden temple prevailed.
Robin Hood entered inside where he was met by shamans and angels, wizards and magicians, and the ascended masters of earth.
He was given a scripture, a picture, a map and a key, a Phurba for the protection of Shambala. The scripture it reads
'The key can only be awarded to those whose heart understands the true meaning of peace.
Those of evil, and those whose minds that chose to be blind, cannot see out of the sea that they are below inside temporarily alive.
Life is a choice will you leave for a new world in tune with the whole of creation?
Or stay below living in a shallow home infiltrated by the dark and unknown?'

As the meditation ended, the chakras of the earth created a new feeling for all those who had been misled. From the mind of the dark magician's lies.
They all jumped on to the bus and travelled to Scarborough Fair to

heal the children whose lives had been tormented into despair.
Before little Miss Riding Hood and her friends and followers, enter the Dragon's den.

Robin Hood handed over his bow and arrow to a man he named King George.
He said, 'I give you my bow and arrow for you are a man of courage to slay a dragon in loves fashion.
Have no fear,
for my words will always be in your ear.
Your intuition will guide you from here.'
He said to his sister you call me if ever you need me, be brave and remember the dragon can't feed from you, or our friends, or your followers,
as you all have the vision from outside of the sea.

Ciao for now, I love you all God bless.

The deadliest disease that flows,
through the human in today's world,
is through the mind
it is called
wetiko telling the mind to lie.
Children are taught not long after birth,
Father Christmas,
the tooth fairy, the bogeyman.
Subtle white lies to keep the child in line.
Programming a lie into a fresh new mind,
creating allowance for this disease to strive.
The lie becomes an unseen addiction,
always needing a new disguise,
to keep the greed chasing part of the mind alive.
That will lead to exhaustion, eventually
your true mind will become forgotten
eventually rotten.
Let go of your lies,
on death you don't want to have an unpleasant surprise.

Dan was running late for Sam,
Dan told Sam to walk to his house
in a different direction,
saying the original path has been shut,
because water had filled it with mud.
It was the middle of summer,
poor Sam didn't even consider
Dan had lied to save himself time.
Sam took a new route
he didn't have a clue
he was led down the wrong path,
with fatal bad luck.

A thug jumped out,
and stabbed Sam in the heart.
Dan's soft lie, cost Sam to die
there is never a need to lie,
even if you think you are saving time.

Dan now forever cries,
every day in his life.

Death and misery became the norm,
arousal of love to the underground became a concern,
as the century turned.
How were humans ever going to learn truth?
If life to the demons in the deep state is no concern.
They would watch us burn,
control the planet and its turn.

Media and schools who only repeat
what authorities
want you to see, not to question the system's belief
or taught to live by integrity and morality.
What is real truth in our history?
Most humans are infected with the deadliest disease,
that runs through mind,
the dark side of the mind *wetiko* lies.
Can it be possible the earth is not hurtling through space at 67,000
miles per hour?
Is the sun really 93 million miles away?
We have never crashed into Mars
we never see new stars, or crashed into a constellation of love.
We have never entered a new Milky Way,
although we are meant to be spinning away.

Could the model be like a Russian doll?
Levels to evolve,
a frequency law?

Nothing is exempt from being disproved.

The greedy devil and its friends to their delight
eat up too much light.
No more life of how we know,
no flying birds,
sailing seas,
dead palm trees,
all of life nearly deceased.
One day the devil and co got full
and could not breathe.
A light shone over their shadows,
the shaman's spell they followed
'well done with your greed,
you have nothing left to succeed'.
Facing its own darkness because it has nothing else to eat.
The scared beautiful souls of love, in hiding
came forward to the voice of the shaman's timing.
Then helped dig the devil's well,
keeping it there with a love spell.

Don't be kept in your
Devil's fight or flight.
The parasite in the mind
that will override
when you leave love behind.
Love in the heart with the divine
will see you past the stars.
Or in a well in an unconditional hell,
left in limbo with no libido.

How much do you care for your soul's enlightened freedom and existence?

What is it you find,
in your subconscious mind?

The dragons, devil, demons, djinns and *wetiko*
the parasite on the mind, friends in evil.
All alive in your waking sleep,
the dark part of the mind
tormenting you to repeat, bad deeds,
cascading your spiritual needs,
to take you along their dark ancient gallery,
sailing along your stream
of your naive consciousness.
Thieving your soul's clear clarity,
stealing your light and honesty,
borrowing its way into one's skull.
Once it overrules the mind's eye,
you find you lie,
forgotten how to cry, no respect for life
justifying your own disguise, lost into a rapid demise until your own
mind is captured and the soul dies.
Show yourself, and others, love
in and outside,
wash the brain. Honest humble stable clean the parasites away
for this is how it dies.
Take control of the subconscious mind
control yourself through love and compassionate fun,
I give you the sound of the starting gun.

To align with divine graduation,
releasing the bad temptations
for you to go to a place of satisfaction,

in a world of unconditional love and unification.
Preparing yourself for all that will come,
for your soul after death will all depend on what you have done.
The universe is not complete until you have played your part the choice is yours for your soul's art. The ascension to Heaven the knowledge of Atum is already inside your heart, do you wish to start?
Life is preparation for death.
Corruption from evil, corrupted alignments.
Hate the undeveloped power of love,
when one is in a state of ignorance
a false bliss will manifest unforgiveness,
that follows one to mental sickness.
You can't expect to complete a marathon without training.
You can't expect to meet the heavenly realms without seeking alignment.
A crying pain, the enslaving spirits
that have been infiltrating
the psyche of those who have been,
neglecting compassionate divine training.
End up in the realm of limbo,
to be infiltrated by fallen angels,
who cut themselves of from God's creation.
Jealousy is jeopardy to seeing true infinity.
Dark spirits that don't seek divine merit,
they perpetrate from the darkest of places.
Failing to prepare is preparing to fail,
for leaving this veil.
No one gets out alive

unless you overrule the serpent
inside.
Preparation to reach the next level,
is all there inside of you to unravel.
Working on yourself and connecting with,
the divine realm,
will steer you clear from the limbo of hell.

All loving religions spiritual mystics can give you the spiritual tools and skills,
to unlock the soul's higher self,
to guide you to the higher realms.
Mathematics can unlock codes,
science can show healthy roads.
Sefirot vessels can fully flow
astrology and nature will show
you patterns,
for you to work on and grow,
what direction to go.
Educate yourself with integrity compassion and courage,
accumulate all the spiritual knowledge
allow yourself to nourish,
for the soul to brightly flourish.
Partnership with the divine breaths,
a healthy mind.
Many people die through the loss of connection with the divine.
To leave this world to enter the limbo of hell.
It may sound harsh,

it's not rejection,
if you were stranded in the middle of
the midnight sea
and had no bright light.
How can you be seen
to be saved and relieved?
Simply left in limbo
with darkness, worry and pain,
who will you call on to be saved?
What you have stored in the subconscious mind
is what you will meet.
Communicate with the subconscious
mind
control the threshold
for the conscious perception,
bring forward healthy ambitions.
Release your hate for this is evil's bate,
not looking after your health is giving the
evil burglar your wealth.
Harm towards others is only harming yourself,
for when you leave this physical realm.

For the divine,
is your greatest friend,
your only friend
In the end.

The shaman's telescope.
Take a look through to your potential future.
Take a look through to the point of death,
see yourself playing life's game of chess,
your up and coming manoeuvre
is where you will go next.
Seeing all of your future choices,
you soon see how you can retune your alignment.

Pull away your eye,
acknowledging all the lies,
change the misconception.
A change of mind a change of direction.

Acknowledge the new perception.
The loved one you could've done more for,
the friend you just left, in selfish neglect,
pain that you inflicted,
the love you neglected.
Become the one who is uplifting.
See life from death, move forward
leaving no heart broken.
If you can't love someone don't hurt them.

The love you withhold is the pain that you will carry.

It was a normal busy day in circus town's
theatrical play.
The blind working endlessly all day
vampires out at night looking for prey
for the vulnerable were tired from working all day.
Generations had passed, minds massaged
as the dragon hid, chuckled and laughed.
The traumatised minds had been shown a deceiving, lifeline.
From the death of the life stealer named
Adolf Killer.
The traumatised were thrown money,
babies came in a hurry,
houses built, holidays in guilt
in summer they rarely felt ill.
The babies born had been taught not to mourn,
made to believe a man called Jesus died so they can sin
unaware their sins come back around
keeping life in fear
bringing them a karmic debt that they may not clear.
Throughout time the babies grew blind
didn't know the difference between a laugh or cry.
On one particular day the blind head circus clown,
Mr Beejay,
announced a bat had shat across the land.
His servant Mr Smallcock squirted into the
blind kids a moisturised prick, part of a ritualistic black magic
potion trick.
Paedophiles believe it's okay to sin

twisting messages the heavens sent.
Their awful lie cost many kids to die.
As the dragon's *wetiko* parasite
hides in the mind, disguised, as the karmic debt will rise,
bat crap, became the towns new lie, to keep the blind in line, for a
heart murmuring time. In came to play
Mr Pricky Mr Ballmalteser, Sir Hardon
penis pleasers,
cleaning the chief's gates from smegma,
supported by the chief of circus police
Ms Dickgreaver
in line with Adolf Killer's hidden
knowledge dissevers Dr Cockswap and Mr Man Bellend.
The core still hidden.
In circus town the blind were made to believe
that the clowns' semen was freedom by coercion
from a penis, all are blind from the *wetiko* virus.
All unknowing the final observer is watching, with the spirits of
love purifying.
Relaying messages back to forgotten God
with precise timing, laying foundations
for the demise that's coming.
Observing candidates,
pencilled in for the sold, soul, scroll, showing
reading circus town's
last theatrical poem.

The demon hunting club
23/19 white socks.
Love spells have been cast
cornering the dark arts.
The shamans, magicians and wizards' traditions, full moon admission, a tear drop of love fell into the rain and mud, ready for when the sun come up. The spirit gangsters went swimming to avoid detection the demons ran, the vampires' fangs withdrew, the fallen angels tried to hide too. The evil became cornered into the view of the moon, as they all looked through. Their minds felt spooked, they were all asked the question.
What to you is truth?
Pull your mind from the demonic dragon's
hijacked world
or be locked inside its AI robots' realm
to whiteness the enlightened end game.
For in time all will come to God to pray.
As love and completion will perish
for those who didn't run away.
How many more times will you be gifted the
light of day?
For you to revaluate the pain, from the play.
Greed and control,
just doing what one was told not questioning the control,
is where the soul is sold.
Pay your karmic debt.
No remorse, is the fool's
Three-legged horse.

The sold souls entered the pitch-black sea,
a harrowing trip until they have learnt unconditional peace.
Awareness of karmic debt, begging for a new heartbeat.
As the divine shaman's net is cast and set,
slowly reeling in the sold souls,
draining out those who await death row,
back to the dark sea they go,
to be added to the register
of the dead soul scroll.
In the divine shaman's realm they are contained,
until repentance is made.
An overwhelming nauseous feeling,
of their own raping displeased abandonment to life.
The sold souls can no longer see.
Only listening to the sounds of others crying in doubt,
unknowing if they will ever come out.
Drained into the shaman's
utensil drum.
The drum is pounded until the sold souls fall out
into the whistling sounds of the
deep underground.
Like crabs they crawl,
selfishly crawling over another,
crawling around
pulled down with pounds
again and again,
until they have learnt from the compassionate realms.
Proof of trust,
can they even be considered,
to be taken from the shaman,
for their soul to be recovered?

A soul is earnt,
if it is sold
it will be captured and filtered into
a very
dark hole.

Angels and shamans await us all
allow your heart to come pure,
for you to be sure
of a golden reward.

Have faith in divine,
not biased infiltrated data-driven humans.
Scars in front of the stars,
fire on Mars.
Mercury's anatomy, astronomy, curiosity, enthusiasm.
Sarcasm from the point of fear.
Water outs fire, evaporation becomes clear.
What way will the consciousness steer?
The dead can still hear.
You can't look back at history and not feel shocked, we can't turn back the clocks.
But we can move forward in love.
The beautiful spirit of Lady Diana is all around us,
sending love from her white doves.
We experience as the individual,
but as a whole
we are one giant family.
We are the Homo sapiens.
The wise primate.

The witness in the tunnel,
was a man with a tache,
pockets filled with cash,
a beard fully attached.

Tall dark and mysterious he stood,
the presence he posed,

was that he knew.

He was the man with the clue.

He said,

'study and watch the moon, understand, absorb the energies that come through
her eye in the sky,
she looks through at night.'

The moral code,
the foundations
honesty, integrity,
that brings a mind to stability.
Compassion for all of life.
Honesty is the greatest attribute you can hold,
and will never see you wrong.
Learn to be grateful
patience will always await the inevitable,
be unique and play the game fair.
Have respect for yourself always,
with integrity, noble morality,
we will see no more, violent catastrophes.
As the generation of change,
be a good example all day,
selfless commitment,
with your own health looked at first,
allow yourself to give and serve.
Putting the needs of others ahead of your own,
you will see your angelic aura grow.
Activating the best of your potential,
moral perfection,
by passing dark temptation,
manipulation.

Allow love to prevail,
you can never fail.

Honest humble stable.

You are not submersible,
now you are magical.

The difference between going left and right,
is that you will see the same place
in a different direction.
The observant ones will always ask
a question.

Be open to suggestion, to those that you question, be wise enough
to not put
yourself into submission,
use the right language and your intuition.
The gloom of uncertainty, the feeling of mystery,
may not always be the same as your history.

Your vision of joy may be held back by your inner child.
But you are more mature than a sacred text.
Sit your inner child on your knee
let them know their mind is mature and free.

An incoming vicious verbal attack arises.
You remain as calm as Floyd Mayweather Jr in his squared circle,
and leave them a few surprises.
You cover up well with sharp timing,
once the attack momentarily passes,
you change the angels of conversation
and find the open mind,
choose your desired angle and land at the precise time.
You start to unravel their aggressive mind,
for their next onslaught you have them caught, they then fall short,
your education is now taught.
Remain calm, sharp, honest humble and stable, tolerance wisely enabled.
50 times out of 50 you walk away like
Floyd Mayweather Jr,
stable and able,
for the next tuition,
you are available.

A man aligned broke free intuitively divine
from his cocoon his higher-self spoke.
To himself and friends, we won't be late for the golden place
for my friends I will always wait.
I will be there for you, any time of day,
make you smile what ever you say.
Help you succeed in the rainy days,
help you no matter the cost
I will always find you, certainly when you feel lost.
And if things get tougher I will never allow you to suffer.
Don't be afraid of who you are
or afraid of speaking out.
Asking questions that may not be
considered as normal.
Keep your mind open to all possibilities
exposing yourself to your deepest fear,
will bring forward freedom and relaxation,
there are no limits,
it's you who creates limits.
Thank you mate for being there for me
we shall be friends for eternity.
We won't be late,
even though there is so little time in this lifeline
we are the descendants from the light.
We always shine throughout space and time
in line with the divine.
Now go fly, be a symbol of peace young butterfly. Now you know we
will never die
nothing can steal our life.

Let's be the two people whose eyes cross,
withhold the stare,
that forces us past others' predatory glare.
Start conversation that brings about childish flirtation.
Separate from our groups who could never walk in our shoes,
go in for the kiss,
no withholding bliss.
Buy street food,
ask what music we both listen to.
Head towards the mountains, with the orange moonlit stars.
We now have a view,
we gasp.
We see life's full existence,
talk about great wonders.
Though it is no great wonder how we got to this moment.
We are the ones who took the chance
with that one glance.
We explore each other's minds,
the unknown, like the night sky.
As we pick a star, travel far into the future,
we see a bright prosperous conclusion
for life's confusion.
We connect our DNA strands to the land with golden plants, that can read our hearts,
washing the patterns of the dark ancestral past.
Soul cleansed, blood washed.
Now free of manipulating spite, our intuition frees to evoke a desired road.
For night meets the day,
we feel the power of love again,
will you take my hand?
I am willing to be your man.

Treat yourself and smile twice.
Buy yourself a treat,
with a smile upon your face.
Put it in a safe place that you rarely go and forget.

And when the timing is right you go back to that place,
you see that treat
that brings another smile on your face.

Treat yourself and smile twice,
you won't have to pay a second price.

Just the illuminating feeling of love and surprise.

Felt an unwanted experience last year,
ready for new experiences this year.

Imagine the protective physical materials around you, as a golden protective blanket.

To protect your aura of light,
from the feelings you may feel at night,
protect yourself with a warm protective jacket,
from the cold bitter lies that you may be told in winter.
Flowing skirts, shorts,
Short-sleeved baggy shirts,
to give yourself breathing space in summer,
see your garments together with your flowing untouchable aura.

A protective waterproof so you can't
drown, in other's despair.
Protection from the yoyos in town,
looking to pull peoples love around.

Rewinding their strings,
because they are not free.

Head into circus town,
and watch all the clowns go up and down.
See their love be pulled, all around
you have your energetic protection,
with your feet now firmly on the ground.

As you are the king or queen of
noble morality shining the magic
with remedy,
go have fun in town
your third eye will see all around.

A Liverpool fan found a café, he was in desperate need
for a toilet,
he walked back up the stairs and felt rude
he hadn't brought any food.
But to the left they had a fridge,
that sold bottles of goods.
He brought a bottle of karma cola,
he immediately thought of
Gianfranco Zola.
A skilful taste of pleasure, he says
people would see it and measure,
towards Coca-Cola.
He said you had to agree what joy it can bring,
you can choose to neglect,
but have respect or
karma will come back and bite you in the neck.
I know this too well,
when I spread hate on Chelsea's great spells,
Liverpool fell.
Thank you karma cola
no need for me to look over my shoulder,
unless I play football against,
Gianfranco Zola.

The story of the revolution of the angry homophobic, racist, confused Chelsea FC football fan.

He would see a woman, to him she was a whore,
at this point in his life he could never score.
He would see a gay man to him he was iniquitous.
He would never say no to Indian food, but despised those in Asian clothes.
Had no love for London pubs, though very fond of Brighton lunch,
hated Magaluf where the girls were loose,
but loved Ibiza, senor, senorita.
He hugged and kissed all the men in town when Chelsea FC were crowned,
the euphoria lifted him off the ground.
One day he came back around and sat himself down.
To himself he had a quiet word,
an epiphany he learns.
He was living the life of a confused clown
in circus town,
he is now aware the clock tower has a new ringing sound.
He realised,
his judgments were purely a product of the environment in circus town.
And his actions were of a very silly clown.
He now walks around town as a ticket tout
for equality and diversity.
Unconditional love, his new philosophy.

The planet of love
where open hearts are shown,
you'll never walk alone.
The hearts of evolved,
for us we will always have one another,
to the rest it's unknown
but open for whenever, the rest wish to come home.
We live in grace
the face of grace is a place,
we always embrace.
Together our love is fun
our history will show, how others can grow.
You'll never walk alone,
on the planet of love
direction to the Holy Spirit above.

Fighters fighting in a compassionate mutual love for the sport,
pain paying for the fighters,
children's futures.

The collective energy of the crowd can turn insane,
a satanic worship of pain.

Life is preparation for death,
we stride towards death on life's process train.
Pride for fighters is the name of their game,
death for them they know is coming someday.

But let's not forget,
the compassion the fighters have mutually met
in an insane way it's a spiritual play,
may they all be blessed with
a healthy fate.

Christopher Livingstone Eubank

an enlightening honour to listen to his
warriors code.

A man rebounded in childhood,
surrounded by deprived alike guys.
He has the knowledge to act in violence
though will only stun a man to silence,
with precision and knowledge within alignment
through his English literature that enlightens.
That will diffuse any situation with no violence.
The former world boxing organisation,
middle and super middleweight
champion of the world.
The spiritual face of combat sport
in true alignment with himself, and the divine.
Should all those who choose, to fight in combat sports
be in an oath of allegiance to his,
warriors code.

For your genuine task in the world is to ensure peace.

The warriors code.
The warrior is strong, yet their sleep is fragile.
Their wisdom,
an amalgamation of precedent,
yet their decisions cannot be based on the frailties of man.
Rather fuelled by divine inspiration ascending from the heart.
They know not anger, and only fear the unknown.
The warrior does not judge, for their true assignment is to deliver evidence of superior behaviour to the creator of man.
The warrior does not dream of frontiers. They only see,
the horizons.
The warrior is a creature of irony, for their genuine task is to ensure peace.
The true warrior knows, accepts, and embraces above all,
Integrity, which is their only weapon and forgiveness,
the one true cleansing virtue.
Only when one can fully absorb these most divine of all virtues,
can one at last see how impossible and futile it is to make war.

Ladies and Gentlemen, Boys and Girls,
those are the spoken words,
of the
most honourable gentleman.

The souls KING of boxing
Christopher Livingstone Eubank.

Connection to the divine covers you in this electric storm,
as you sail along in the sounds of the electric song,
you learn your soul is forever long.
When you awaken
your soul,
sat behind the orbital cavities,
intuitive electricity,
activates the heart and pineal gland
with love and prosperity,
removing the self-made captivity
taking control of your creativity,
to a personal destiny.
As the speed picks up you learn to hover,
amongst the electric blizzards rain
you have cover,
in the wilderness of pain,
love is always met with appreciation,
in this electric play.
Allowing the mind and body to move,
open and freely.
Introducing manifestation,
expanding yourself with
enlightening thoughts and knowledge.
In the wilderness you now find yourself in,
is enlightened, self-made courage.
Flourishing the sefirot vessels
the knowing of God,
your fear is forever gone.

The home of homes,
inside the sanctuary home,
watching reborn shows.
Looking back through the electric storm in the,
akashic memory,
universal epiphany,
today is the place to be great,
for we are all lucky to be given the light,
of day.

After assembly,
what role do you wish to participate,
in the role of creation
in the universal play?
God a musician what string do you take?

She was locked into the frequency
found,
she knew no different
from her parents conditioning grounds.
To her at this moment in life.
Life was what it is, no care no gifts.
Gifts and kisses, if someone gave her presents everything was
pleasant.
She was living the life of a rich peasant.
Then one day her soul awoke to repentance
when she saw her boyfriend's reactance
to her selfish actions.
A change in her brain's inductance
created a new electrical current,
and all of a sudden she realised
she hadn't been abundant to those who love her,
because her frequency had been aberrant.
Her new electric feel
bypassed the feelings of ill
and awoken to a compassionate skill,
she saw her parents' conditionings
as a low band frequency of naivety,
of not accepting the 99% of visible light
that we cannot see.
She came to the awareness that life is more,
when you except the reality
that there is plenty more out there.
Worlds of invisibility, to all of the creativity

she made a connection to the
Christ consciousness,
changed her frequency with simplicity,
now part of the universal prosperity
an awareness to the higher self,
ready for her to meet her full potential
in this life she was dealt.

Two lost souls in a lost realm
in a desperate plea went to see
the oracle witch, who lives behind
the golden gracious palm trees.
They asked her to read their palms, to see if they can be free from their minds' displease.
To life they want to succeed.

She took their palms.
She said it's simple your suppression is an inevitable transformable part of your awakening to the love you have been withholding.
Feel the trees listen to the breeze listen to your hearts beat, to learn intuition to guide you with please.
Connect yourselves to nature
question everything question yourselves question the stars.
Let go of your guilt it will make you ill,
let go of greed and you shall be free.
Repay those with care, by sending out a love prayer, to those who you made feel in despair.
Connect with the divine for a healthy mind.
What I can see is that you will come to be in a place of noble morality,
becoming a symbol of peace for those in need.
Stroke my tropical iguana pet lizard, and into your mind you will see the wizard,
who will stay with you, and guide you when life feels a blizzard.
For when you meet the shaman
you are in line with the divine ambition.

Little Miss Riding Hood and her friends and followers who the Pegasus commended, were walking through the dragon's den, on route to Rupes Nigra.
In the arms of unconditional love to see the sunset begin.
Into a rainforest they walked, to come out to the other side to see the sun shining.
Suddenly they saw lying a wounded golden dragon on the brink of death dehydrated and very little breath.
They all looked at each other and questioned what motives this dragon may have.
Little Miss Riding Hood spread the dragon's wings and saw on his chest an orange-gold gemstone, her intuition told her and she said out loud. This is a dragon of prosperity, she asked one of her followers to pass the barrel of Holy Water that they got from the wizard's well.
She poured some water into her hands and fed it to the dragon.
Almost instantly the dragon was healed then got up and flew away.
Suddenly they were approached by a group of armed men with guns, knives, masks and a deadly grin,
wicked women in sin, with snakes' skin.
The dark night dragon's servants.
They said we can't let you past to see the sunset begin, because we have the key
that will let you in.
As we can't be let in because us men and women are mentally ill with the lying *wetiko* disease.
She asked, life is a choice why do you choose to lie?
They replied, will you lie and pretend to die?

Little Miss Riding Hood replied, no but my Pegasus can fly when
magic is in the sky and the stars align.
Why would I lie and pretend to die?

The group of armed men said, well if you pretend to die, we can say
we have found love inside and that our hearts don't lie because we
saved a life, because we want to go over to the other side.
She asked, can you cry to show me your love in and outside?
The armed men and wicked women
all looked at each other and started grinning.
They said, gives us your heart and the Pegasus wings,
and you can have the key,
just say please.

Little Miss Riding Hood and her friends felt really uneased they
turned back around
into the rainforest's muddy grounds, the crossroads they had found
they all sat down and said what now?

They lit a candle and said a prayer
the flame grew a flare
out of the flame came the shaman at the crossroads, he was there.

His words were clear.
Tell the thieves why you are here.
Me and the angels stand with you, the psychic trees will breeze,
they freeze if need.

So little Miss Riding Hood and her friends and followers went back
and told the thieves why they had come to see the sunset begin.
The armed men cocked their weapons the women slithered, towards them,
they snatched little Miss Riding Hood
and tried to run away
suddenly the trees shivered,
King Arthur's spirit endeavoured and hovered.
The thieves froze, it started to snow,
the golden dragon reappeared, his wings created a blizzard.
Suddenly the dark night dragon appeared on top of the mountains
and descended towards little Miss Riding Hood and her friends and
followers in one last attempt to steal all of their souls.
King George aligned Robin Hood's bow and arrow and shot it into
the heart of the dark night dragon, and slayed him with the sword
of compassion.
It created a fire trapping the dragon's empire.
Little Miss Riding Hood brushed off the thieves and quickly took
the key,
as the sunset started to begin
down the hill to the beach to see,
the golden gate of peace,
which the jaguars and lions guarded.

They took a look at little Miss Riding Hood and her friends and
followers' souls
to read their sins.
They asked did you lie to the thieves today? They all said no,

the jaguars smelt their souls, not one
fell down.
They asked did you steal?
Little Miss Riding Hood fell.
She said, I stole because I didn't wish to call my brother Robin to steal their hearts because I wish to learn strength by myself. This way love now has a spare key and can't be taken by another set of thieves.
Now these thieves live in the freezing world of anxiety until they learn not to lie and thieve.
Now they are trapped, the dragon can't feed from the deadly thieves as King George shot my brother's bow and arrow
that was embedded with love remedies, now the dragon's heart has to restart back in the dark as it is trapped in its own fire with the sold souls it stole.
It no longer has a key,
so it can no longer manipulate and try and hide and disguise the golden gate of peace.
The jaguars run around in circles then rolled on to their backs in complete pleasure and laughter,
the lions' roar echoed for humanity.
Little Miss Riding Hood came off her knees,
the sun had set on the horizon from a view from the golden beach the silhouette of the new moon arose,
the Pegasus wings grew
the stars connected, the angels and the Pegasus flew,
a magical beautiful view,
the shaman looked from behind the golden gate of peace

and said, come on over and open up, and walk straight through.
The sun and moon aligned a transparent eclipse.
The creation of a new sun
they all walked into the moon,
through into the sun.
Directed by the Pegasus to the star Osiris
for the ascension through to the other side of life, purified minds
into the divine realms,
and there it was the golden key of alchemy.
Prosperity the remedy
for lives who felt pain and suffering inside,
and didn't choose the dark side of life.
Those who aligned with the laws of compassion
unconditional love to life,
perfection inside the temple.
You may feel you are in jeopardy
but the shaman's promise to you,
pay your karmic debt
in will come prosperity to the world left behind.

Everything,
now starts to become heavenly.

The three wise men travelled through the universal glen
to align the souls of peace and prosperity,
for the initiation of the universal king,
to be aligned with the queen.

You are a success because you resonate honesty and peace,
in a world that heavily deceives
bleeding in greed.
You are the good omen of belief,
To open up eyes to the heaven's cries for the wise to ignite the
universal peace.

Atum aligned.
Ra shone his light, from his eye
into the king's head.
Illuminating his eyes
his chakras span releasing his ram,
protecting the lion lamb,
protecting the children who lead the peace.
Awarding the senses,
the falcon he gave for sight
the dove so all can be touched
fruits and grapes so all can smell and taste,
an angel so all can hear loud and clear
the planet and nature
to connect with the divine pulse.
An intuitive eye
so all can read the true meaning of the starry skies.

The gift the king was given,
awarded the heavens
the ability to open eyes
to release all the lies,
from prisons built inside.
To bring forward life
without the disguise
to free all from hate and suicide.
Showing how precious the importance is to every single life force.
The deliverance of natural healthy food allowing all to survive.
Purified spring waters, life's main supporter,
no abstract for greed.

A bright prosperous future,
for life God and nature
the symbol of 3 becomes alive in all the souls' minds.
Seeking alignment for life's assignment.
Breathing through the tree of life,
to allow the eggs and seeds to be relieved.
To acknowledge all the
pain inflicting over the centuries.
The dead and sold souls, shown the life they have thrown.
The children shown, how that life
could never fully grow,
an intuitive mind to never allow life to fall back into that demise.

For in time, the branches fall
the collective consciousness drawls.

Fills up in a bag and splits and empties like quicksand.
To lay foundations for revelations
that only love will show and grow,
for you to know the true road,
peace for life has been chosen.
Evil, left all alone.
To never come back into the home.
the purified king and queen inside the individual arose.

The shaman felt the unconditional love at first sight, she had one deep
blue and one deep brown eye, golden skin,
lips that had never sinned.
'Come in and join us,' she said, we are the whistlers, the sound of
freedom, the channel to enlightenment.
These are my friends, Ian the channeller, Maria the mystic, Chris the
light bearer, Silvana the dream catcher,
Debbie the spirit guide,
Linda the healer.
And I am Heaven,
we come from the seven sisters.
Our stars are bright, take our hands and we will show you our version
of night.
In between his eyes came this bright light,
in simultaneous directions
he had visions of what can become,
worlds to see, souls to free.
Their night was a vessel of light,
with an aroused feeling of self-righteousness,
their children were all taught
to stand tall, with the highest appreciation of God's compassionate law
even those who were born small.
For they are the world that is to become.
They had taken on the task to travel through Orion's stars,
took some elements from the planet Mars, to
then teleport through the great pyramids of Egypt.
To whistle a tune to the shaman's drum,
from the sound of a flute

a soft and sacred harmonious tune
that will be heard and sung
to the vibration of love.
Renavigating lost souls,
healing all of life inside
helping them find their way outside.

For the truth to been seen and arise,
shifting the cosmic view with the frequency penetrating through.
The conscious sea pushed the winds to align the symbol of 3,
accompanied by the shaman angels, wizard and magicians
as the consciousness meets the spirit of please a compassionate plead.
The flight of the birds,
the crickets chirped, the wolves howled
Jaguars purred, the lions roared,
let go and freed.
All that's left was we, with the spirit of nature, compassion we feed.
In the universal mind that watches over the earth in a shamanic view
throughout time.
As the Holy Spirit comes in
to see alignment of the souls
the spirit breaths an ablution for the purified illumination to breathe
again a new fusion of eternal life into the purified minds.

One starry night on the horizon of the cosmos,
sat on a rainbow,
were all the ancient philosophers
who had walked the earth,
gathered together as a group of friends.

They all had different perspectives.

Waiting to speak to the divine, one thing depends,
will they all stay friends?

They all await their turn,
first come first served,
some still in need,
some so pleased.
They did all agree life is a way to grow harmoniously.

The divine's words to the group
'I am what I am and I have a plan'
the philosophers all stayed friends
and asked

'Can we all be part of life's restart?'

Some asked can you recycle me even as a
palm tree,
so we can relearn to breath?

An ancient scroll was sent back home to the spiritually awakening world.
The beginning is the end,
the end is a beginning,
the planet's tradition, spiritual admission.
To a new world that can only be revealed when guilt and greed is let go and freed,
war no longer forms, harm no longer caused.
New stars in front of Mars, new moon.
A sentient harmonious, musical tune,
to play out across the view
of the ascension into this new room,

your self-revelation is coming soon,
the revolution inside of you.

This is the story of,
Jewish rabbis, synchronist mystics,
druid priests and priestesses,
shamans and angels,
ancient pharaohs
the heavens sent.
Loving souls of the dead.
Hindus bringing the union of mind,
the Muslims' crescent star showing
progression and time,
the ankh cross unlocking the stars,
opening hearts,
all those in favour of love together at last.
Navigated by the dharma wheel,
all sailing together in an abundance of love.
Giving the final goodbyes to the dark times.
The crystal ship
sailing past the
heavens' stars.
For us to fully understand our
beautiful given land,
resting on solid bedrock,
flowing water and sand,
nature flowing all in sync.
For in this story,
we are born to die,
for us to grow.

The middle symbolises
life's prime time,
to grasp the sight of life.
For the evolved souls
the path is clear,
directing us to the conscious sea
all aboard heaven's sailing ship,
towards a new frequency,
to a world that has never been seen
in perfect timing leaving the
horror scene.
For the hearts and minds of love,
perceiving the new view,
everything becoming apparent
to the souls of God.
Ein Sof,
infinite paradise
with an open plan.

There was a ship found in the centre of
of a land-locked rock.

With no sea no record of human loss.

But one man,
containing in both of his hands,
magnets of equal light and dark energy,
ready to connect the source to prosperity.

Leaving the technology for those who were ready.

The connection was made,
that brought out change,
brought out the sea,
so he could now leave.
He shouts,

'I leave you with peace and prosperity,
along with free will,
but if you destroy this new world
you will live in guilt.'

Let's create our new legacy,
become the souls of peace and prosperity
in the new garden,
a game of snakes and ladders,
now we have escaped the dragon.
In line with the divine,
we know the final outcome
the light that shines, we climb towards
in time.
Together we slowly creep towards the top
when one of us drop
we build back up.
With a kiss of life
to breathe in the golden light
to help understand the mischief of our minds,
that sent us back down
to the lower grounds
to regrow the love,
in this compassionate realm,
to understand the true nature
of the prosperous creator.
Cuddling behind a rock
with the feeling of being in love.
Sharing each other's growth
entwined with nature,
growing the finest of fruit vines
keeping us pure to life,
no such thing as time.

Knowing you love me how I love you,
breathing together in nature's endeavours
attempts of being strong forever,
for the moment we are now in
we are the strongest ever.
My twin flame 11:11 the symbol came
I will always love and care for you.
We enter the top of the kingdom's castle
so we can create new worlds in the skies,
for our soul group's children to shine.
As we watch side by side we move stars through our voice. To form
their light to bring the children to physical life,
that rhymes in beautiful sounds of chimes.
For when we depart the children become the restart, a reincarnation
of our soul's art
we will never be torn apart.
I love you my twin flame my love for you is the name of the game.
Goodbye
We will see our selves alive again one day just in different symbols.
In a new burning flame.
The
end
=
the energy never dies.
I promise you your soul will fully grow,
as I travel on to the end of my growth,
our detachment is the best
for us both,

to fully understand growth
to get back home alone.
For at the purist point of the God head
we become one with the divine light.
So we can reincarnate the shine,
to rejoice back with the twin flame,
in another game.
When we see each other's face
taking shapes in symbols of grace,
we know our souls
are in the right place.

As we rejoice in prosperity,
holding hands through golden gates.
The divine gives us everlasting infancy for us to awaken the maturity as we align our purity to be guardians of life's code of existence.

I love you.

The Holy Spirit Atum came in.
I therefore make you my loyal king and queen,
I give you my magic, power, strength and wisdom
for your achievement on capturing the serpent,
that was bent on destroying forever.
Look through Ra and Hathor's eyes
for the eclipse to rise in line,
as you now shine bright through
the dark sky's new beginnings of life.
Aligned and divine, now crowned,
into the divine house of wisdom.
Your crown the serpent you captured,
a snake that can no longer escape.
You are both now a safe keeper of life.
For my love of you I give to you,
a life to choose, for your wisdom,
are the rules you wish to use.
Align with me your view, of a world of good,
for the children to grow up in fun
living under your sun.
Your wisdom with the magic I give
will arrive the skies.
Your tears of joy will drop as purified water
into your golden bowl.
A sprinkle of stardust to lay foundations,
to settle as land for the water of your tears
to flow into lakes and streams
to reflect the sky's uprise.

For the souls ready to enter
your golden bowl
who vibrate on the vibration of both your souls.
Building teleport pyramids for the frequency
to flow.
One deep breath in. One deep breath out,
and the pulse of life connects to the frequency found.
Create nature for the children's connection to the pulse will be greater.
Seeds available from the high priests, grow as you please.
Luxury of golden palm trees jungles with no deadly disease.
To build amongst for the children to sleep
for the sound of nature is what they will see.
For their decoding of dreams are their reality
for coding a no show of jeopardy
for the protection of the universal prosperity.
For whatever your intuition resembles
for the children to use as magic protecting symbols.
Integral compassion enables a well behaved stable.
The lion's roar symbolises strength and protection
the jaguars detect deception, telepathy with your creation.
The monkeys to swing in freedom
the cattle eat the grass in ration
to recycle life in good fashion,
the birds to fly to show their minds' direction,
for whenever there's a new inception.

You call me when life has grown to the maturity that all of life is in
the purified code of eternity.
A proud moment to see when they have
their golden epiphany.
The children of gold become the masters
of the
universal code,
that only they shall know.
Holding the secrets of the Gods attaining all knowledge in sacred
secret symbols for the future, keeping our sacred wisdom, alive and
hidden.
To teleport back to the
divine house of wisdom,
to be met with the highest order of appreciation,
the guardians of life's code of existence.

And for you my great king and queen
come with me, and I will show you
everything,
and why this is all meant to be.

The universal dream while every one's asleep,
the consciousness is taken on a journey
to a bright new light in the soul's life,
a total eclipse, to a morning of bliss.
An awakening of the sanctuary
the gateway to divine kingdom,
for those who overcome their darkest of thoughts
that the dragon had brought.
The long-awaited peak
no longer games of hide and seek.
A place of freedom the old world's mind becomes obsolete
a knowing of no repeat,
a free home your allowed to roam to get to your throne
lands to grow natural flow,
with synchronistic floors
perishing the old contaminated show
that then folds in on itself alone.
A moment of darkness inside the dream arose.
The eclipse created a vessel to the other side of the sun,
for the banks of conscious energy to break a river of gold to flow.
The consciousness
connected back to the universal minds,
the dream awakens at the perfect time
awakening the blind, who lived with an
honest heart throughout their time.
The spirits of love
directed by doves,
directing nature, wildlife, combined,

to an awakening breath of life,
for the spirits of love of mankind.
The rebirth, the new side of the light's golden eye,
the sky's evolved a purification
that shines bright inside, the eyes of life
in the last deep sleep
the universal dream
that all of love came to see,
all sailed into life alive,
together
with divine connectivity.
Inside the universal code of
peace and prosperity.

An artificial intelligence controlling computer system on this planet earth,
is being created without knowing.
I call on the masters of the tech computer world,
to programme the algorithm,
with the meaning of
compassion
with the intentions being directed to the meaning of love.
Unconditional love is to drive technology,
use the computer to remind us of what we truly are and that is love.
As the human spirit ascends,
to a new evolution process,
we can use the computer
but not to see it as the prime salvation,
the computer is a creation of man.
Ultimately it does not have a soul it cannot care for man like a human can.
But can help us understand the structure of man or remind man if going off task.

If let loose to run,
the extinction of man,
will become,
twenty seventy-nine may not show.
The way you wanted it to go
for those who choose to
God will be with you.

The task for man,
nature to be treated like the prime creator,
understand the truth of one's self
and the life force it was blessed.
The evolution of unconditional love,
for all of life,
will bring about a reason for our existence
cultivating real freedom through the awareness of truth.
Self-knowledge will always surpass limitations,
and bring about a coming of maturity.
We create ourselves,
we are our own historians,
the directors of our future.
Take responsibility, call on your integrity,
for life's remedy,
so the next generations can have celebrations.
Peace and prosperity.

INSPIRATION
MANIFESTATION
GROWTH

HEALTH
WEALTH
HAPPINESS

HONEST, BIRTH
HUMBLE, LIFE
STABLE, DEATH

3 6 9
GEOMETRY LINES
THE VORTEX SHINES

Take the greatest of care for your mind,
and health.
Life is all potential that offers opportunities
the choices you make are down to you,
we all have free will.
All actions have consequences.

The only time you look down at a human,
is to give them a hand up.

Send them politely on their way,
if one is led astray
Mr and Mrs Misanthrope
may want you to flop.
Keep your head up
because you will reach the top,
in the highest realms of unconditional love.

Be your best, leave no karmic debt,
you are the best open secret
you are love and respect.

Part 4

The Symbol of 3.

In numerology the number 3 represents:
Social interaction
Creative self-expression
Optimism
Tolerance

Social interaction: amongst us humans it is a vital part of our natural growth and development of communication skills, whether it be sign language, spoken language or body language. A constant flow of social interaction, certainly from a young age helps create an open and curious mind and will prevent social anxieties. If a child is locked away for lengthy periods of time in their formative years the child runs the risk of social disorders as they enter young adolescence, that will then likely follow them for the rest of their lives. If social interaction is taken away you create stress, depression, confusion, anger, anxiety. You only have to look at prison incarceration statistics and the recent lockdowns to help understand this. Since the lockdowns the world's violence has sorely increased, along with self-inflicted deaths. In the United Kingdom the biggest killer in men is suicide. Where I lost both my father and uncle and very nearly myself, all of whom served in the British Army. Young uneducated, and unaware of the fact that all the wars my father and uncle fought in, it would never bring peace to either side of the conflict. The suicide statistic is sickening and is rocketing among our women, this in its own right is a pandemic. Potentially this will become a worldwide phenomenon. For the times we are in, have a look through your phone book and call to a friend, you may not have spoken to for a while, uplift people bring a smile to someone's face. People normally only phone you or speak to you because they want something. Something as simple as this can be the big difference in someone's mental health. You never know it may just enlighten them to do something great for the world, that was brought about because of the love and appreciation you gave.

Creative self-expression: adopting this into your life in any form of creativity, whether it's music, poetry, art, painting, writing, fixing something with odd bits, building sandcastles, writing uplifting messages on stones, anything. It can help you in many ways, whether unloading a lifetime of depression. Getting rid of built-up emotions, looking for an answer in something, getting rid of anxiety, or even to help you sleep. If you are someone like me and dream a lot and especially if you are suffering with nightmares I find writing them down and using it for a storyline then adding a happy ending extremely powerful and mind opening. I see dreams as a gift, don't let them drift. I have had many dreams that have given me answers to the reality we live in, and to questions I wanted answers for. I also use creative self-expression to alter my state of consciousness. Help to see life from a different point of view. Opening the mind to all possibilities will allow the beauty of magic to run fluently into your life. And please certainly allow it into your child's life, they are the future the 20s babies and beyond will be a new breed but it will be up to us to allow them to succeed.

Optimism: indoctrinating optimism as a mental state, and believing that nothing you do, be seen as failure, and that life is a learning experience, seeing the brighter side of things, you find that you will experience more positive events. My optimism for the future, for all of us on earth is with confidence that we will wake up to our spiritual calling. I do believe we will turn the dark to light, and all live in an era of universal peace. But this all comes by each individual taking responsibility for their actions, with the use of critical thinking, and believing in one's self. Each day I'm starting to hear people ask more and more questions. Asking questions comes from curiosity, curiosity is a great thing, don't shut it off. If answers are not always found this creates an opening for the expansion of the curious mind to grow. A question can open the mind. With your mind open, and with honest morals, you will always be in control of it.

Tolerance: there are different types of tolerance depending on the area of life it is reflecting. In terms of your mind and emotions how many times have you been able to tolerate someone's bad behaviour before you've gotten them out of your life? A long time for many. Just because you may be tolerant to bad behaviour towards yourself does not mean you should allow this behaviour to carry on in your life. Eventually you will come to that realisation, and find the courage to do what is right for you. People have only so much resilience towards unjustified behaviour. Connect tolerance with calmness and intuition, and you will find the wisest outcome you desire.

In the angelic realms the symbol 3 represents:
Inspiration
Creation
Manifestation
Growth

Inspiration: is something from within and we have all used it. At this moment you may not feel inspired at all. And if you are looking for some take your mind back to the last time you were inspired to do something new. For some that may be when you wanted to find a new job, get fit, learn a new trade, drive a car or even tie a shoelace, anything. Take yourself back to that moment you felt inspired to do something new. Sit there and really feel and embrace that moment, not when you achieved it but when you wanted it and were inspired to get it. And relive it in your mind until you really feel back in the moment. Then remember how it felt when you achieved it. Coming to the realisation that the power is still within you to achieve again and that you are successful. Lifting your vibration to allow inspiration to filter through. Do this for just a few minutes a day then allow for your mind to completely rest and come to a place of stillness. Then go on a nice walk through nature, or just around your block, and I assure you something will filter into your mind and inspire you.

Creation: we are all part of a creation whichever way you wish to look at it, being born from a mother is a creation in its own right. I believe in a divine god, Atum, there are many different names for the creator of life. I don't believe God at its purist form has a gender, but can manifest itself into a male or female if wanted as every single living organism is part of the creation so it is within all beings. Everything is Atum if you look for God in the physical it may never be seen, if you look with your mind it is all around. You see the universe as a gigantic work of art surrounded by mysteries that takes the curious mind to infinity, ask to illuminate your awareness to grasp the supreme being. Many have just never bothered to connect properly and to be guided. I am not affiliated to any religion. But take the spiritual and positive aspects from all of the wonderful teachings from all scriptures and that they all have a part to play in God's creation to bringing enlightenment. Most speak in the same language as me and that's love and compassion. Just because some faiths differ in certain stories it doesn't mean you can't connect with the true meaning of life, which is to become at peace with one's self and with others. I read most of the stories in the religious scriptures as symbolic. I find it helps find the true meaning of the stories and not take it all too literally. Many wars in our history have been fought. Any man or women who decides to kill another man or women in the name of God is sadly very lost and misled. The world's media have done a very good job in dividing people and religious groups playing them off against one another. Yes, life is very tough at times, but this is not the divine God's fault. We are here to learn and overcome ourselves and I totally get it when people say, 'Well, there can't be a God because look how awful it is here.' If you have read my book fully I have answered this symbolically. Believe me I had a hard time with my relationship with God for a long time, trying to understand why life can be so painful. So I prayed respectfully and repeatedly and compassionately and was given many answers through dreams, manifestations and connection through channelled writing. You will be very surprised with the power of prayer. We are all creators, certainly if you have children you have created a life. We create ideas in our minds that lead us to creating and manifesting outcomes in our lives. So as humans if we have lost our spiritual centre and get totally caught up in the world of materialism of course this will lead people to not believing in or feeling a divine energy. We then become more likely to create negative experiences that then lead to negative outcomes.

Manifestation: you are the magician the king or queen of your mind and body. Nobody controls your soul, only you. You can manifest whatever you want, operating on the frequency of love with positive optimism. You will manifest whatever you want in your life a lot faster and see your pathway in life a lot clearer once you have sent out a clear and positive message to the divine, and it will arrive to you at the right time. Whatever you are focusing on you will manifest into your life, where attention goes energy flows if your thoughts are negative you will manifest negativity if they are positive you will create positive manifestations, keep your mind in control, by bringing the loving heart and mind to centre.

Growth: in life we grow both physically and emotionally we grow an awareness through consciousness. Although your physical growth will at some point stop, your emotional growth and consciousness is never ending, but for some you may've shut this off at a preadolescent. How many man-children do you know? Or child-like women who are at middle-age? Emotional growth is emotional intelligence. Growth and the expansion of the mind's consciousness is always readily available, all you have to do is open your heart and mind and remember you only see 0.0035% of visible light. If your ready built-in belief system feels like it's being attacked learn to trigger your mind to be open without judgement, this doesn't mean you have to agree but allow information to be absorbed so you can then reflect and look at things from different angles, helping create a wiser answer or approach. Expanding the growth of your emotional consciousness and awareness will open up new doors to new worlds. You will then start to clearly see opportunities, new ways of living, a healthier way of being both mentally and physically, which you once locked yourself out from.

3 is the key to all of your magic.
It is the number to which the meaning,
all was given the number of wholeness.
Harmony, wisdom, understanding
life's three-part process
birth, life, death,
past, present, future
beginning, middle, end
your life is solely for you
master honest laughter
live life leaving no regrets,
no karmic debt.
Take all the opportunities that life has to offer, that inside feels right
and honest for you
make the most of your loving tune,
whilst striving towards your full potential.
Allow the symbol of 3 to be your key to your soul's freedom to
enlightenment,
I give you, and you give yourself and others the permission
to be happy and free mentally,
along with the greatest of
health, wealth and prosperity.

I love you all God bless x